More Biblical Quilt Blocks

New Inspirational Designs

Rosemary Makhan

Martingale®
& COMPANY

More Biblical Quilt Blocks:
New Inspirational Designs
© 2005 by Rosemary Makhan

That Patchwork Place® is an
imprint of Martingale & Company®.

Martingale & Company
20205 144th Avenue NE
Woodinville, WA 98072-8478 USA
www.martingale-pub.com

Printed in China
10 09 08 07 06 05   8 7 6 5 4 3 2 1

Library of Congress Cataloging-in-Publication data is available upon request.
ISBN 1-56477-581-X

Mission Statement

*Dedicated to providing quality products
and service to inspire creativity.*

Credits

President: Nancy J. Martin
CEO: Daniel J. Martin
Publisher: Jane Hamada
Editorial Director: Mary V. Green
Managing Editor: Tina Cook
Technical Editor: Ellen Pahl
Copy Editor: Sheila Chapman Ryan
Design Director: Stan Green
Illustrator: Laurel Strand
Cover and Text Designer: Regina Girard
Photographer: Brent Kane

Dedication

Other things may change us, but we start and end with family.
—Anthony Brandt

To my family

Ken: Our son, for the memories, your wonderful artwork, and the valuable lessons you taught us about empathy and the afterlife, we'll be forever grateful. We love you and miss you.

Candice: A wonderful daughter, friend, and kindred spirit. Thank you for your thoughtfulness, generosity, and kindness—you're an inspiration to us.

Chris: My left-brained husband who keeps us centered and on track. With your talent and love for gardening, you create a little bit of paradise for us to enjoy here on earth.

Acknowledgments

I give thanks with a grateful heart to:

Jill Pettit at Jillybean's Pride in Oakville, Ontario, for offering the Sacred Threads class. Also to Josie Abel, Chris Forster, Erika Gyger, Patricia Harris, Sharon Nicholls, and Corry Smit for taking the class and sharing their quilts in this book.

Sue Patten, for her excellent machine quilting skills and for fitting my quilts into her busy schedule.

International Textiles Ltd. of Richmond, British Columbia, and Telio & Cie Textiles of Montreal, Quebec, for supplying some of the fabrics used in the quilts.

Nancy Martin for suggesting the idea for this book; also to everyone at Martingale & Company who worked on this book for their encouragement, enthusiasm, and expertise.

CONTENTS

INTRODUCTION

Nancy J. Martin could not have known, when she asked me to write this book, how much I needed this meaningful purpose to my life at a most difficult time. Making the quilts and writing this book have been a healing experience and another step in my journey as I attempt to draw closer to my source.

I'm very grateful to all of you who shared your letters and stories of how making quilts from *Biblical Blocks* had such a depth of meaning in your lives. It has made me realize that these quilts are not only an avenue for creative expression and an opportunity to showcase our workmanship, but making them is therapeutic during troubled times, comforting when we are sad, healing when we are grieving or despairing, and a source of joy when our hearts are glad.

Bible studies can be based on the themes represented by the quilt blocks in this book, such as Road to Paradise, Joseph's Coat, and Jacob's Ladder. These quilts can be used as friendship or memorial gifts, wall hangings for churches, fund raising, charity, and personal enjoyment.

My hope is that the quilts will have very special meaning for the makers and will enrich their lives as well as the lives of those who view them or receive them as gifts. It has been an epiphany for me to realize that through my quilts I can not only help others but also create messages of appreciation for such things as spirituality and nature. I hope to put this newfound knowledge to use in my personal growth as a quiltmaker when I am designing and making future quilts.

Through our quilting we can all help to make this world a better place.

Rosemary Makhan

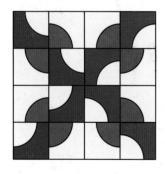
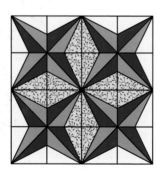

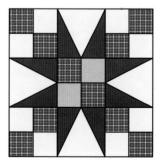

Crown's Secret Exposed
by Patricia Harris, 37" x 38"

When Patricia placed four King's
Crown blocks together, she noticed
a secondary pattern, which she colored
to feature a hidden maze and a sunburst
surrounding the center.

Sacred Threads Eighteen-Block Sampler
by Josie Abel, 72" x 90"

Josie, a student in my Sacred Threads class
in Oakville, Ontario, chose to use a narrow
sashing to frame her blocks in this on-
point setting. The sashing helps define the
blocks since Josie used the same fabric for
the background of all her blocks.

*Sacred Threads
Thirty-Block Sampler*

by Sharon Nicholls, quilted by
Sue Butzer, 82½" x 96½"

This is Sharon's first full-size quilt.
Although she found the class
challenging, she especially enjoyed
learning how to draft patterns and
construct the blocks. The beautiful
batik fabric used in the sashing and
border helps to unify the blocks
into a harmonious whole.

Sacred Threads Twenty-Block Sampler

by Chris Forster, 78" x 92½"

Chris plans to use this quilt in her guest
bedroom. She quilted Bible verses
into the borders of her quilt for
her guests to discover.

Garden Walk

by Patricia Harris, 51½" x 51½"

Patricia created a secondary pattern
in her quilt by varying the colors
in the block. This variation created
a subtle inner circle and medallion
center in addition to the stars.

Cross within a Cross

by Chris Forster, 84½" x 96"

Chris made this quilt on
impulse at the end of the class
to use up leftover hand-dyed
and batik fabrics. She varied
the pattern by using
half-square triangles instead of
squares in the corners to create
a more pleasing overall design.

A View of the World
by Patricia Harris, 24" x 24"

Patricia drafted an 18" Christmas Star
block to showcase this charming cardinal
print that she found in her stash.

Golden Threads
by Erika Gyger, quilted by
Carol Cunningham, 82" x 101"

Erika used a plain block
between her pieced blocks
so she could feature a lovely
quilting pattern.

The following directions cover all the techniques needed to construct the blocks shown in this book and to assemble them into a quilt top. I've also included finishing instructions that will guide you as you complete the steps to turn your quilt top into a quilt.

Fabric Selection

Use good-quality, 100%-cotton fabrics that have been washed and ironed. Test any dark-colored fabrics that might run; wet them separately in a basin and if there is any color seepage into the water, treat them with a fixing agent such as Raycafix.

Most of the projects in this book are made using a wide variety of fabrics. Collect fabrics in each color that vary in value, scale, and type of design. Search through your fabric collection and then shop for fat eighths and fat quarters until you have at least four to six variations in each color range. Your quilt will be much more interesting to the viewer, and an added advantage of having multiple fabrics of the same range is that if you run out of one of your fabrics, you can substitute another and it will never be noticed!

Vary the background fabrics as well as the design fabrics to add secondary interest and visual texture to the overall appearance of the quilt. Keep within the same basic ecru color range, but use fabrics that are different enough to be noticeable. Varying the background fabrics looks especially nice when you are making a block-to-block quilt, such as "Thirty-Block Sampler" (page 69).

Design Wall

I cannot emphasize enough the importance of a design wall. Things can look amazingly different when seen from a distance instead of up close. Place your fabric options on a vertical design wall when choosing the fabrics in your blocks, sashing,

set pieces, and borders. It is almost essential when determining the placement of the blocks in your quilt. Try to stand far enough back from the wall to see the overall effect of your quilt. Looking through a reducing glass or camera lens can further emphasize any changes that should be made in your choices as you proceed with your quilt.

Cutting

Rotary cutting is recommended for most cutting, but you will need to make templates for some shapes that have irregular measurements. All rotary-cutting measurements and all templates include ¼" seam allowances. It is of utmost importance to be accurate with your cutting measurements.

Glad Tidings

For blocks with intricate shapes or long slender points, it's helpful to spray starch the fabric to give it more body before cutting out the pieces.

Making Templates

Template patterns for the pieced blocks are numbered and grouped following the directions for the quilt projects. They begin on page 87.

1. Trace the template patterns onto transparent template plastic to make durable, accurate templates. Mark the lines with a fine-tipped permanent marker that will not smudge.

2. Mark the template number and grain-line arrow on each template. The grain-line arrow indicates that the template should be placed so that the arrow lies straight along the lengthwise or crosswise threads of the fabric. The other edges of the template may be on the bias or at an angle.

Some blocks require the reverse of a template, indicated by the word "reversed" in the cutting directions. To reverse a template, simply turn it over so it's upside down when you trace around it.

Templates can also be used as rotary cutting guides; put tape on the ruler to mark the cutting line by placing the ruler over the template to obtain the measurement. To avoid confusion, draw an arrow on the tape pointing to the side that should be cut.

Sewing Accurate Seam Allowances

It is of critical importance to sew an accurate ¼" seam allowance. If this is not done, the blocks will not fit together, and this will affect the size of everything else in the quilt, such as the alternate blocks, sashing, setting pieces, and borders.

Test your ¼" seam by cutting three strips of fabric, 1½" x 3". Sew these strips together along their long sides. The middle strip should measure exactly 1" wide. If it does not, your seam allowance needs to be adjusted until this measurement is obtained. Place a piece of masking tape or moleskin ¼" to the right of the needle on your machine as a guide, or adjust the position of your needle.

When sewing blocks that require templates or have unusual shapes, you will not line up the edges of the cut patches. You will need to line up the seam intersections instead. To prepare these pieces for accurate sewing, mark a tiny dot (on the wrong side of the fabric) at the point where the seam lines intersect. Measure ¼" in from the cut edges of the fabric piece, draw the seam lines, and mark a dot where the lines intersect.

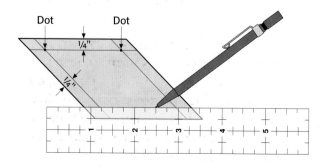

A Quilter's Quarter Marker tool is particularly helpful for marking seam intersections (see "Resources" on page 95). This tool contains all the angles commonly found on cut pieces. Place the tool over the wrong side of your cut piece so that the fabric edges line up exactly with the edges of the tool. Then push a mechanical pencil through the hole and gently twist to leave a dot. This will enable you to get a perfect match. It will also ensure that you have a ¼" seam allowance extending past the points on your block so that when the blocks are sewn together, your points will not be cut off or lost. If the mechanical pencil does not show up on your fabric, use a fine-tipped blue or white water-soluble pen.

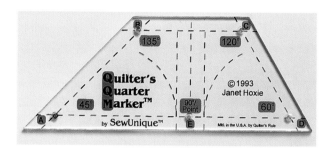

Quilter's Quarter Marker

Glad Tidings

Use fine pins with small heads to match seam lines; long pins with big heads create a "drag," which can pull the fabrics and create a mismatch.

Set-in Seams

Set-in seams are seams with inside corners or angles that require two separate stitching lines. Many of the star blocks have set-in squares and triangles. These seams must be stitched in two stages, starting and stopping ¼" away from the end of the seam line.

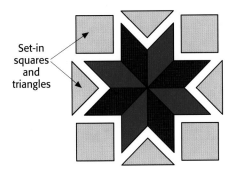

Set-in squares and triangles

1. Mark a dot (on the wrong side of the fabric) at the point where the seam lines intersect, referring to "Sewing Accurate Seam Allowances" (page 10).

2. When aligning the pieces to be stitched together, match the dots on each piece. The seam starts and ends at a dot. Backstitching is done to secure each end. However, if one end of the set-in seam lies at the outside edge of the block, do not backstitch; sew to the end of the seam.

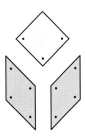

Paper Piecing

Paper piecing is an accurate way to stitch pieces with sharp points, such as the star points in Garden Walk (page 38) and Road to Paradise (page 53). It is also used for Hosanna (page 45), King David's Crown (page 50), Job's Troubles (page 47), and Storm at Sea (page 63).

Grain line is not as important in this method as in traditional piecing because the paper gives the block stability during sewing. Use a #90 sewing machine needle (this larger needle perforates the paper better), thread in a color that will blend, and a smaller-than-usual stitch length (approximately 12 stitches per inch). You want the paper to be easy to tear away but you don't want your stitches so small that they are difficult to rip out if you make a mistake. You can use ordinary paper for the foundation or purchase paper specially made for paper piecing. You can also use freezer paper. The wrong side of the fabric will adhere to the shiny side of the paper when pressed, adding stability and increasing accuracy.

1. Trace and cut out the paper pattern for the block you will be making. Cut it out slightly outside the cutting line—you will trim the fabrics to leave an exact ¼" seam allowance on the paper pattern after the stitching of each section is completed.

Pressing Points

Pressing seams as you sew is important for accuracy and precise piecing. Follow these pointers for best results.

- In most cases, press the seam allowances toward the darker fabric to prevent the seam allowances showing through to the quilt top.

- Be careful not to stretch seams or bias edges when pressing. Lift your iron with an up-and-down motion rather than sliding sideways.

- Press so that you create opposing seams (one seam faces left and the other faces right) at intersections; this way the seams will nest together, and matching points is much easier.

- Where a lot of seams come together, it is best to press the seams open. In many of the star blocks, pressing the seams open makes the blocks easier to sew and they will lie flatter. When joining a quilt "block to block," matching is often much easier when the seams are pressed open.

2. Cut fabric pieces or strips approximately ¾" wider and ¾" longer than each section or patch on the paper pattern.

3. Begin with the patch numbered 1. Place the first fabric piece, right side up, on the back side of the pattern (the side without any lines). Hold the paper up to the light to make sure that the fabric piece extends over the edges of the shape by at least ¼" inch all around.

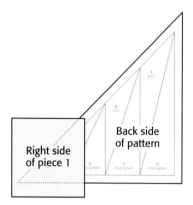

4. Place the second fabric piece, right sides together, over the first fabric piece. Hold them up to the light to make sure that you have left ample fabric on all sides to cover the B shape plus at least a ¼" seam allowance all around.

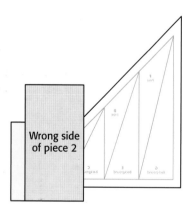

5. With the marked side of the paper foundation up and the fabrics on the bottom, stitch on the line between pieces 1 and 2. Begin sewing two

or three stitches before the line and continue one or two stitches past the line so that the seam will be secure.

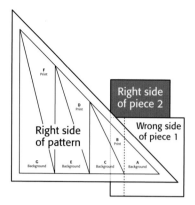

6. Open up the patches and press.

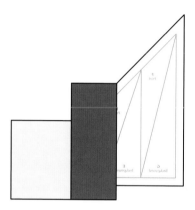

7. Fold the paper pattern back and trim the seam to a scant ¼" or less.

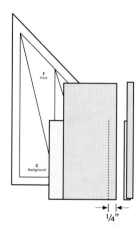

8. Fold the paper back along the next seam line. Trim the fabric so that it extends ¼" past this fold line. This trimming creates a straight edge upon which you can line up your next strip, making placement much easier.

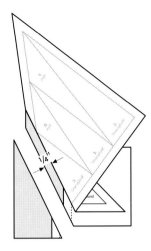

9. Continue in this manner in numerical order until the pattern is completely covered with fabric pieces.

10. Use scissors or a rotary cutter to trim away the excess fabric around the unit, leaving a ¼" seam allowance all around.

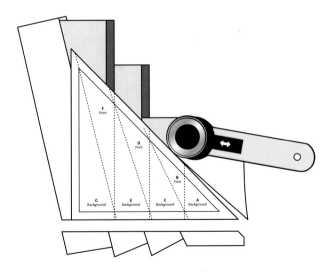

11. Leave the paper pattern in place until after you join the completed units to make the block. Then carefully tear away the paper.

For more detailed directions on paper piecing, see *Show Me How to Paper Piece* by Carol Doak, listed in the Bibliography (page 95).

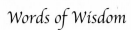

Words of Wisdom

Baste the units together to make sure the points match before you sew them. Once you sew the units together, the small stitches are difficult to rip out.

Freezer-Paper Appliqué

I use appliqué to stitch curved pieces like those in Solomon's Puzzle (page 57) and the "Coat of Many Colors Quilt" (page 80).

1. Trace the appliqué pattern onto the dull size of freezer paper. Cut the freezer paper along the drawn lines. Do not include seam allowances on the freezer-paper shape.

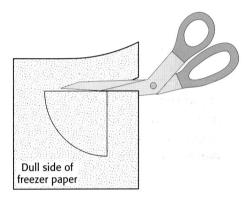

Dull side of freezer paper

2. Iron the freezer-paper shape onto the wrong side of the chosen fabric. Cut out the fabric leaving ¼" seam allowances all around the freezer paper.

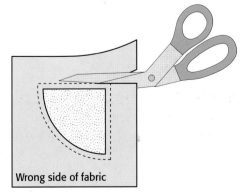

Wrong side of fabric

Cut ¼" away from freezer paper shape.

3. Using a fabric glue stick, place a small amount of glue along the curved edge of the freezer paper. Glue the curved seam allowance to the edge of the freezer paper. Do not clip the seam allowances because this will weaken the seam.

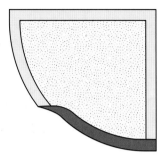

4. Place this piece on the background fabric as directed in the block pattern or quilt instructions. Appliqué the curved edge to the background fabric by hand with a small invisible stitch or by machine with a very narrow zigzag stitch and .004 monofilament nylon thread.

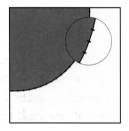 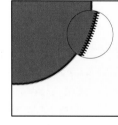

Hand appliqué   OR   Machine appliqué

5. Cut away the background fabric underneath the appliqué shape, leaving at least ¼" of fabric for the seam allowance. Use a spray bottle to lightly mist the seam allowances with warm water to dissolve the glue. Gently remove the freezer paper using tweezers. Press.

Borders

Borders create the frame around your patchwork and appliqué, much like a frame around a piece of art. I like the look of mitered borders, but you can use either straight-cut or mitered borders depending on your preference.

◇

Words of Wisdom

It is always wise to measure your own quilt before cutting any borders.

Straight-Cut Borders

These borders are a popular choice because they are the easiest to construct and take less fabric than mitered borders.

1. Measure the length of your quilt top through the center (the outer edges of the quilt can stretch with handling and pressing). Cut two side border pieces this length.

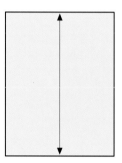

2. Mark the centers of each border piece. Pin them to the quilt top, matching the centers of the border pieces to the center of the quilt top edge. Pin the ends and ease in any excess fullness.

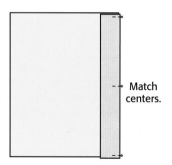

Match centers.

3. Stitch with a ¼" seam allowance. Press the seams toward the borders.

4. Measure the width of the quilt top including the side borders. Measure through the center as you did in step 1. Cut two border pieces this length.

5. Pin and stitch to the top and bottom of the quilt as in steps 2 and 3.

Mitered Borders

Beautiful borders with corners that meet at an angle make the perfect frame for any quilt top. Follow these steps to add borders with mitered corners to a quilt.

1. Measure the length of your quilt top through the center. Add two times the width of your borders plus an additional 3" to 4" to this number and cut two border pieces to this length. Measure the quilt top crosswise through the center, add the same amount, and cut two border pieces to this length.

2. Find the center of the side border strip by folding it in half and marking it with a pencil. Measure out from the center in each direction a distance equal to one half of the length of the quilt top. Mark these points. Mark the same points on the top and bottom borders, using one half the width of the quilt top.

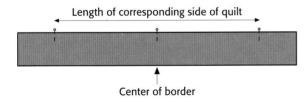

Length of corresponding side of quilt

Center of border

3. Pin the center of the border strip to the center of the side of the quilt top and pin the marked points to the corners. Pin the remainder of the border to the quilt top, easing as necessary. Sew the border strip to the quilt top, stopping ¼" in from each corner. Backstitch to secure

the seam. Repeat this step for the remaining three border strips.

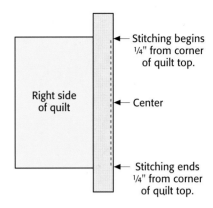

Right side of quilt

Stitching begins ¼" from corner of quilt top.

Center

Stitching ends ¼" from corner of quilt top.

4. Fold the border strips at each corner so that they meet at a 45° angle. Press the border strips so that a crease line is formed at each corner.

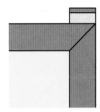

5. Pin the border strips together at the corners, matching up the crease lines. Start at the outside corner and sew inward to meet the stitching at the inside corner of the quilt top. Backstitch to end this seam.

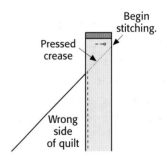

Begin stitching.

Pressed crease

Wrong side of quilt

6. Check that the seam is correct and lies flat. Trim the seam allowance to ¼" and press open.

7. Repeat steps 4, 5, and 6 for the other three corners.

Finishing

When the quilt top is done, you're ready to move on to the final phase of quilting and binding. Take as much care in doing this as you did with the piecing. Choose hand or machine quilting depending on the time you have and the end use of the quilt.

Preparing the Backing

The backing should be at least 2" larger all around than the quilt top. For quilt tops that are larger than approximately 38" to 39" square, you can either piece a backing from lengths of 42"-wide fabric or use special backing fabric that comes in wider widths, such as 60", 90", or 108", so that the backing will not have any seams.

If you piece the backing, make sure that the joining seams do not lie at the center of the backing. I like to split a single width of fabric and sew one half of it to each side of a full width of fabric to avoid a center seam. Quilts are often folded in half for storage, and a center seam in the backing can result in a very distinct crease line in this area of a quilt.

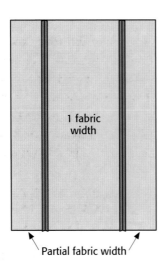

1 fabric width

Partial fabric width

Batting

I prefer a batting that is 80% cotton and 20% polyester, such as Hobbs Heirloom or Cotton Classic by Fairfield. These battings give the look

and feel of an antique quilt, which I love! They are also easy to quilt through and wash very well.

For hand quilting, I preshrink the batting by soaking it in my laundry tub and then squeezing all the water out by hand. I lift the wet batting carefully by placing my hands underneath it and then dry it in the dryer. This preshrinks the batting and makes it much easier to hand quilt.

For machine quilting, I do not preshrink the batting because it looks nice when it shrinks after quilting—it adds more texture to the quilt and more of a hand-quilted appearance.

Basting the Layers

You will need to layer and baste the backing, batting, and quilt top together for quilting.

1. Tape the backing right side down on a flat surface, such as a floor or large table, so that it lies flat and stays taut.

2. Lay the batting on top of the backing, smoothing it out so there are no wrinkles or creases.

3. Lay the well-pressed quilt top, right side up, on top of the batting. Thread baste the three layers of the quilt together if you will be hand quilting. Use a long darning needle and white thread. Baste with safety pins for machine quilting. Baste in a grid, both horizontally and vertically, spacing the basting lines or pins 4" to 6" apart. Begin in the center of the quilt top and work outward toward the sides.

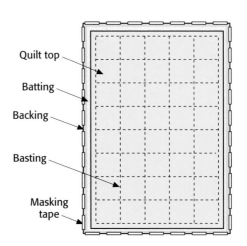

Quilt top

Batting

Backing

Basting

Masking tape

Attaching the Binding

The binding strips for the projects in this book are cut 2¼" wide on the straight grain of the fabric, either crosswise or lengthwise.

1. Cut enough 2¼" strips to go around the perimeter of the quilt plus 12" to 14" more to allow for joining the seams and mitering the corners. Join the binding strips end to end with a diagonal seam. Trim the seam to ¼" and press open.

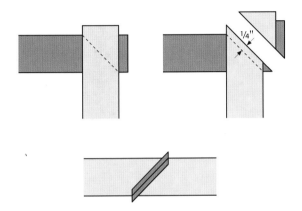

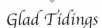

2. Fold the binding in half, wrong sides together, and press to make a folded binding that is 1⅛" wide.

◇

Glad Tidings

It's easier to sew the binding to the quilt before trimming the quilt batting and backing; you can hold onto the fabric more easily, and puckers will be less likely to form on the back side of the quilt.

---

3. Start sewing the binding onto the quilt along one side, leaving a 2" tail of binding free when you start. Use a walking foot and sew a ¼"

seam through all the layers of the quilt. Keep the raw edges of the binding even with the raw edge of the quilt top. Stop sewing exactly ¼" from the next corner of the quilt, backstitch, and cut the thread.

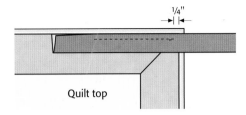

Quilt top

4. Fold the binding up so that the raw edges are in line with the raw edges of the next side of the quilt top. If the quilt has a mitered border, make sure the diagonal fold on the binding lines up with the mitered corner seam on the border.

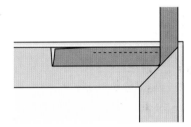

5. Fold the binding back down on itself, even with the edge of the quilt top; this forms a little pleat at the corner, which will later form the miter. Begin stitching ¼" in from the edge, backstitching to secure. Repeat this process at each corner of the quilt and continue stitching until you are about 3" from where you started.

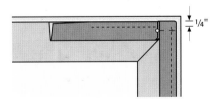

6. Stop stitching and remove the quilt from your sewing machine. Fold the binding strips back where they should meet and mark this place with a pencil.

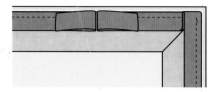

Mark where the strips meet.

7. Sew a straight seam on the line you marked. Trim the seam to ¼" and finger press it open. Put the quilt back in the machine and sew the remainder of the binding.

8. Trim the excess batting and backing even with the edge of the quilt top.

9. Fold the binding over the raw edges of the quilt. Hand sew the fold of the binding to the back of the quilt so that the fold just covers the previous row of machine stitching. Fold the miter at each corner of the binding and slip-stitch in place.

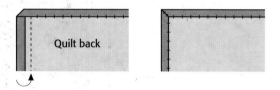

Quilt back

Attaching a Hanging Sleeve

If you plan to hang your quilt, sew a hanging sleeve, or casing, along the top edge of the backing. Make the hanging sleeve from the same fabric as the backing, if possible, so that the sleeve will hardly be noticeable on the wrong side of the finished quilt.

1. Cut a strip of fabric that measures 9" wide x the width of the top of the quilt. With wrong sides together, sew a ½" seam along the long edges to form a tube. Press this seam open.

2. Hem the raw edges at the short ends by turning under ¼" and then 1". Press and then stitch the hems in place.

3. Press the finished sleeve, centering the seam in the middle of one side. Place this side of the sleeve against the quilt backing. Slip-stitch the sleeve in place along the top edge of the quilt back after the quilt is bound. Be careful to stitch through only the backing fabric and batting rather than all the way through to the front side of the quilt.

Adding a Label

Be sure to add a label to your quilt. Stiffen a piece of fabric with fabric sizing or press a piece of freezer paper to the wrong side. Use a fine-tipped permanent marker, such as a Pigma .03 mm pen. Include the name of the quilt, your name, your town, and the date. Add any other information that would be of interest. You can add verses from the Bible or embellish with flowers, birds, vines, etc. After you have finished, heat set the ink by pressing over the label with a hot, dry iron on the cotton setting.

Glad Tidings

Use your computer to print the label in a script-like font. Then trace it onto your fabric using a light box.

BLOCK GALLERY

The blocks in the block gallery are presented in similar colors and values. I've shown them in shades of red, green, tan, brown, beige, and ecru—the colors I used in the "Thirty-Block Sampler" (page 69). Ecru is very similar to beige, but just a bit lighter. It is the fabric that I use as the background in the blocks. Beige fabric is part of the block design. Of course, feel free to use the colors you like best.

After each sewing step, press the seam allowances open or in the direction indicated by the arrows. Pressing the seams open will eliminate bulk where many seams come together and is easier for a block-to-block setting.

The size of each block after piecing is 12½" x 12½", which means that each finished block will measure 12" x 12" after being sewn into your quilt. It is a good idea to measure your blocks after sewing to make sure your seam allowances are accurate and that your blocks are all the same size.

The eight-pointed star blocks are the most time consuming and require very precise stitching because of the set-in seams. I recommend starting with easier blocks that have fewer pieces and progressing to more intricate blocks as your experience and skills increase. The eight-pointed star blocks are Bethlehem Rose (page 21), Carpenter's Wheel (page 23), Heavenly Stars (page 43), and Star of the Magi (page 61).

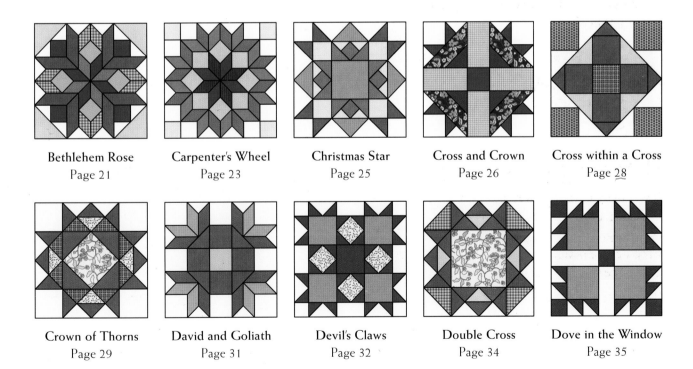

Bethlehem Rose
Page 21

Carpenter's Wheel
Page 23

Christmas Star
Page 25

Cross and Crown
Page 26

Cross within a Cross
Page 28

Crown of Thorns
Page 29

David and Goliath
Page 31

Devil's Claws
Page 32

Double Cross
Page 34

Dove in the Window
Page 35

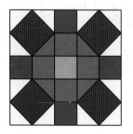

Garden of Eden
Page 36

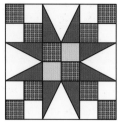

Garden Walk
Page 38

Golgotha
Page 39

Heavenly Problems
Page 41

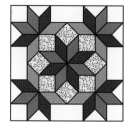

Heavenly Stars
Page 43

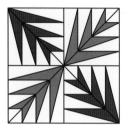

Hosanna
Page 45

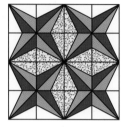

Job's Troubles
Page 47

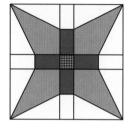

Joseph's Coat
Page 48

King David's Crown
Page 50

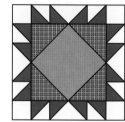

King's Crown
Page 51

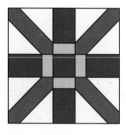

Road to Damascus
Page 52

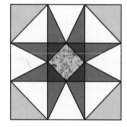

Road to Paradise
Page 53

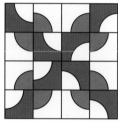

Robbing Peter to Pay Paul
Page 55

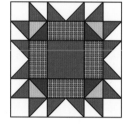

Solomon's Puzzle
Page 57

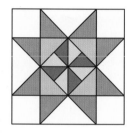

Solomon's Star
Page 58

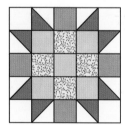

Star and Cross
Page 59

Star-Crossed Christmas
Page 60

Star of the Magi
Page 61

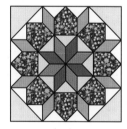

Storm at Sea
Page 63

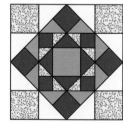

Temple Court
Page 65

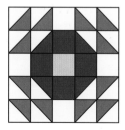

Wedding Ring
Page 67

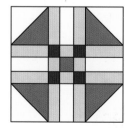

Whither Thou Goest
Page 68

Bethlehem Rose

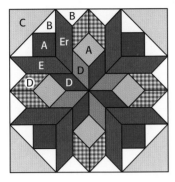

Finished size: 12"

When Herod the king heard this, he was troubled, and all Jerusalem with him; and assembling all the chief priests and scribes of the people, he inquired of them where the Christ was to be born. They told him, "In Bethlehem of Judea; for so it is written by the prophet: 'And you, O Bethlehem, in the land of Judah, are by no means least among the rulers of Judah; for from you shall come a ruler who will govern my people Israel.'"

Matthew 2:3–6

 Note: This is one of the more challenging blocks in the book. You might want to gain experience with easier blocks before making this one.

Cutting

PIECE	FABRIC	NUMBER TO CUT	SIZE
A	Red print	4 squares	2¼" x 2¼"
	Beige print	4 squares	2¼" x 2¼"
B	Ecru print	4 squares	3¾" x 3¾"; cut twice diagonally to yield 16 triangles
C	Tan print	2 squares	4⅜" x 4⅜"; cut once diagonally to yield 4 triangles
D	Dark red print	4	Template 1 (page 87)
	Medium red print	4	Template 1
	Green check	8	Template 1
E	Green print	4 and 4 reversed	Template 2 (page 87)

Sewing

1. To make the center star, make four chevron units as shown below, using the dark red and medium red D diamonds. Stitch in the direction of the arrow, stopping ¼" from both raw edges. Backstitch. Press all the seams open.

Make 4.

2. Sew the chevrons together into star points, stitching in the direction of the arrows and stopping ¼" from both raw edges. Backstitch. Press the seams open. Fan out the seams around the center point to reduce bulk.

3. Referring to "Set-in Seams" (page 10), add a beige A piece between the four sets of star points, stitching in the direction of the arrows. Begin and end stitching ¼" from the raw edges at both the inner corner and outer point as indicated by the dots in the square. Backstitch.

4. Make four chevron units, using the green check D diamonds. Stitch in the direction of the arrow, stopping ¼" from both raw edges. Backstitch. Press the seams open.

Make 4.

5. Sew the units from step 4 to each square at the outer points of the center star, stitching in the direction of the arrows. Begin and end stitching ¼" from the raw edges at both the inner corner and outer point as indicated by the dots in the square. Backstitch.

6. Make four corner units, following the piecing diagram and using red A, ecru B, and tan C pieces.

Make 4.

7. Make four chevron units, using the green E pieces. Sew and press as you did in step 4.

Make 4.

8. Sew the units from step 7 to each corner of the star unit, stitching in the direction of the arrows.

9. Add the corner units to the center star and inset the remaining ecru B triangles along the sides where indicated. Stitch in the direction of the arrows.

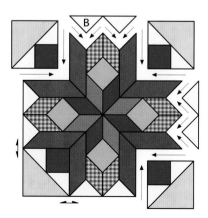

Carpenter's Wheel

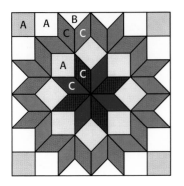

Finished size: 12"

And on the Sabbath he began to teach in the synagogue; and many who heard him were astonished, saying, "Where did this man get all this? What is the wisdom given to him? What mighty works are wrought by his hands! Is not this the carpenter, the son of Mary and brother of James and Joses and Judas and Simon, and are not his sisters here with us?"

Mark 6:2–3

Note: This is one of the more challenging blocks in the book. You might want to gain experience with easier blocks before making this one.

Cutting

PIECE	FABRIC	NUMBER TO CUT	SIZE
A	Tan print	4 squares	2¼" x 2¼"
	Beige print	8 squares	2¼" x 2¼"
	Ecru print	8 squares	2¼" x 2¼"
B	Ecru print	2 squares	3¾" x 3¾"; cut twice diagonally to yield 8 triangles
C	Dark green	4	Template 1 (page 87)
	Dark red	4	Template 1
	Medium green	12	Template 1
	Medium red	12	Template 1

Sewing

1. To make the center star, make four chevron units using the dark green and dark red C diamonds. Stitch in the direction of the arrow, stopping ¼" from both raw edges. Backstitch. Press the seams open.

Make 4.

2. Sew the chevrons together, stitching in the direction of the arrows and stopping ¼" from both raw edges. Backstitch. Press all the seams open. Fan out the seams into a circle at the center to reduce bulk.

3. Referring to "Set-in Seams" (page 10), add a beige A piece between each set of star points, stitching in the direction of the arrows. Begin and end stitching ¼" from the raw edges at both the inner corner and outer point as indicated by the dots in the square. Backstitch.

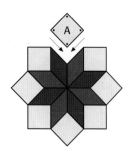

4. Sew a medium red C diamond to a medium green C diamond as shown. Stitch in the direction of the arrow; begin and end the stitching ¼" from both the raw edges. Backstitch. Make eight red/green chevron units and four green/red chevron units.

Make 8.   Make 4.

5. Join the chevrons from step 4 to the center star as shown, setting in the seams as in step 3. Each unit will be sewn and joined to the next one with set-in seams. Press the seams open.

6. Join eight ecru B triangles and 4 ecru A squares where indicated by the arrows in the diagram. Set in the seams as before.

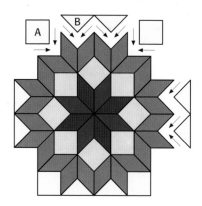

7. Sew the remaining four ecru A squares to four tan A squares. Stitch one of these units to each corner, setting in the seams, to complete the block.

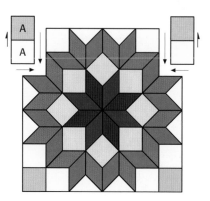

Christmas Star

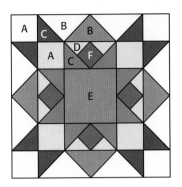

Finished size: 12"

When they had heard the king they went their way; and lo, the star which they had seen in the East went before them, till it came to rest over the place where the child was. When they saw the star, they rejoiced exceedingly with great joy; and going into the house they saw the child with Mary his mother, and they fell down and worshiped him.

Matthew 2:9–11

Cutting

PIECE	FABRIC	NUMBER TO CUT	SIZE
A	Light beige print	4 squares	2½" x 2½"
	Ecru print	4 squares	2½" x 2½"
B	Ecru print	2 squares	5¼" x 5¼"; cut twice diagonally to yield 8 triangles
	Tan print	1 square	5¼" x 5¼"; cut twice diagonally to yield 4 triangles
C	Red print	4 squares	2⅞" x 2⅞"; cut once diagonally to yield 8 triangles
	Green print	4 squares	2⅞" x 2⅞"; cut once diagonally to yield 8 triangles
D	Light beige print	2 squares	3¼" x 3¼"; cut twice diagonally to yield 8 triangles
E	Tan print	1 square	4½" x 4½"
F	Brown print	4	Template 3 (page 87)

Sewing

1. Sew two light beige D triangles to adjoining sides of a brown F piece as shown. Make four.

Make 4.

2. Sew a red C triangle to each short side of the units made in step 1. Make four.

Make 4.

3. Sew two units from step 2 to opposite sides of the tan E square.

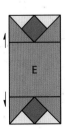

4. Sew a light beige A square to each end of the remaining two units from step 2.

Make 2.

5. Sew the units from step 4 to opposite sides of the unit from step 3 to complete the center star.

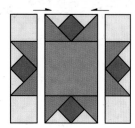

6. Sew an ecru B triangle to each short side of a tan B triangle. Make four.

Make 4.

7. Sew a green C triangle to each end of the unit from step 6. Make four.

Make 4.

8. Sew an ecru A square to each end of two of the units from step 7.

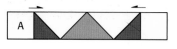

Make 2.

9. Using the completed units, assemble three vertical rows as shown and join the rows to complete the block.

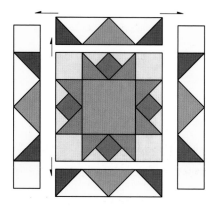

Cross and Crown

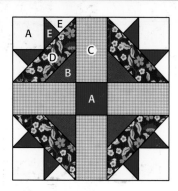

Finished size: 12"

Must Jesus bear the cross alone,
And all the world go free?
No, there's a cross for ev'ry one,
And there's a cross for me.
The consecrated cross I'll bear
Till death shall set me free;
And then go home my crown to wear,
For there's a crown for me.

From the hymn "Must Jesus Bear the Cross Alone?" by Thomas Shepherd and George N. Allen

Cutting

PIECE	FABRIC	NUMBER TO CUT	SIZE
A	Ecru print	4	Template 4 (page 87)
	Red print	1	Template 4
B	Brown print	4	Template 5 (page 87)
C	Tan check	4	Template 6 (page 87)
D	Brown floral print	4	Template 7 (page 88)
E	Ecru print	8	Template 8 (page 88)
	Red print	8	Template 8

For rotary-cutting options, see the template patterns on the pages listed above.

Sewing

1. Sew the red and ecru E triangles together as shown. Make four and four reversed.

Make 4.　　　Make 4.

2. Sew an E unit and an E unit reversed to adjoining sides of an ecru A square. Make four.

Make 4.

3. Sew a brown B triangle to a brown floral D piece as shown. Make four.

Make 4.

4. Join a unit made in step 2 to a unit made in step 3. Make four.

Make 4.

5. Assemble the units, the red A square, and the tan check C pieces into three vertical rows. Join the vertical rows to complete the block.

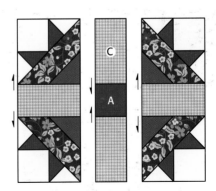

Cross within a Cross

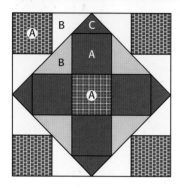

Finished size: 12"

Let us also lay aside every weight, and sin which clings so closely, and let us run with perseverance the race that is set before us, looking to Jesus the pioneer and perfecter of our faith, who for the joy that was set before him endured the cross, despising the shame, and is seated at the right hand of the throne of God.

Hebrews 12:1–2

Cutting

PIECE	FABRIC	NUMBER TO CUT	SIZE
A	Green print	4 squares	3½" x 3½"
	Red plaid	1 square	3½" x 3½"
	Red print	4 squares	3½" x 3½"
B	Tan print	2 squares	3⅞" x 3⅞"; cut once diagonally to yield 4 triangles
	Ecru print	4 squares	3⅞" x 3⅞"; cut once diagonally to yield 8 triangles
C	Green print	1 square	4¼" x 4¼"; cut twice diagonally to yield 4 triangles

Sewing

1. Sew a green A square to a green C triangle. Make four.

Make 4.

2. Sew two units from step 1 to opposite sides of the red plaid A square.

3. Sew two tan B triangles to opposite sides of a unit from step 1 as shown. Make two.

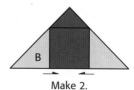

Make 2.

4. Sew the units made in step 3 to opposite sides of the unit made in step 2 to complete the block center.

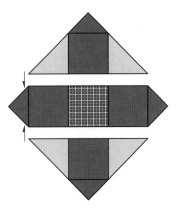

6. Sew two units made in step 5 to opposite sides of the center unit. Repeat with the remaining two units to complete the block.

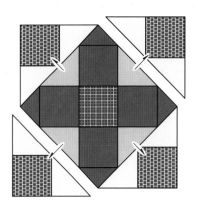

5. Sew two ecru B triangles to adjoining sides of a red print A square as shown. Make four.

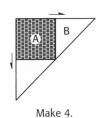

Make 4.

Crown of Thorns

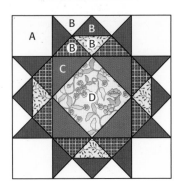

Finished size: 12"

And they clothed him in a purple cloak, and plaiting a crown of thorns they put it on him. And they began to salute him, "Hail, King of the Jews!"

Mark 15:17–18

Cutting

PIECE	FABRIC	NUMBER TO CUT	SIZE
A	Ecru print	4 squares	3½" x 3½"
B	Light red small-scale print	1 square	4¼" x 4¼"; cut twice diagonally to yield 4 triangles
	Green print	3 squares	4¼" x 4¼"; cut twice diagonally to yield 12 triangles
	Red plaid	2 squares	4¼" x 4¼"; cut twice diagonally to yield 8 triangles
	Ecru print	2 squares	4¼" x 4¼"; cut twice diagonally to yield 8 triangles
C	Red print	2 squares	3⅞" x 3⅞"; cut once diagonally to yield 4 triangles
D	Light red large-scale print	1 square	4¾" x 4¾"

Sewing

1. Sew two red C triangles to opposite sides of the light red D square. Repeat on the remaining two sides.

2. Sew a light red B triangle to a green B triangle. Make four.

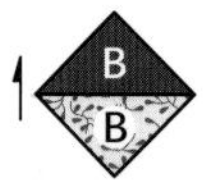

Make 4.

3. Sew two red plaid B triangles to adjoining sides of a unit from step 2. Make four.

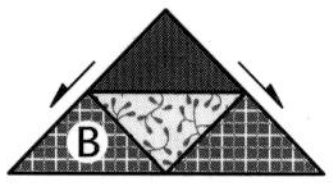

Make 4.

4. Sew an ecru B triangle to a green B triangle. Make four and four reversed.

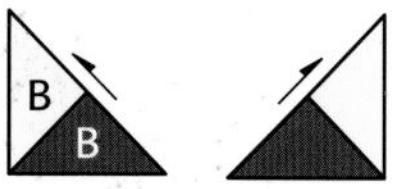

Make 4 of each.

5. Sew two units from step 4 to the unit made in step 3 as shown. Make four.

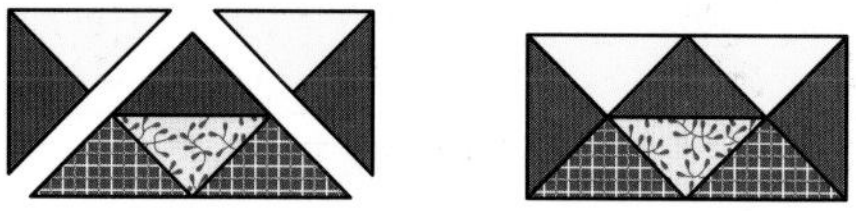

Make 4.

6. Sew an ecru A square to each end of two of the units made in step 5.

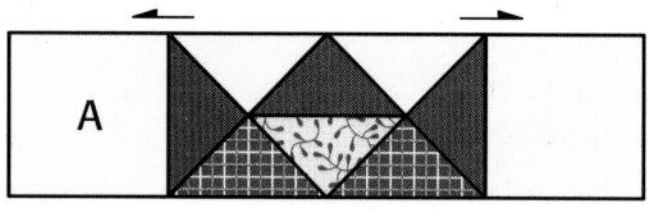

Make 2.

7. Sew all the completed units together to make three vertical rows as shown. Join the rows to complete the block.

David and Goliath

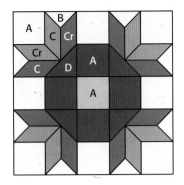

Finished size: 12"

And there came out from the camp of the Philistines a champion named Goliath, of Gath, whose height was six cubits and a span. Then David said to the Philistine, "You come to me with a sword and with a spear and with a javelin; but I come to you in the name of the Lord of hosts, the God of the armies of Israel, whom you have defied." And David put his hand in his bag and took out a stone, and slung it, and struck the Philistine on his forehead; the stone sank into his forehead, and he fell on his face to the ground.

1 Samuel 17:4, 45, and 49

Cutting

PIECE	FABRIC	NUMBER TO CUT	SIZE
A	Ecru print	8	Template 4 (page 87)
	Medium green print	4	Template 4
	Beige print	1	Template 4
B	Ecru print	8	Template 8 (page 88)
C	Light green print	4 and 4 reversed	Template 9 (page 88)
	Red print	4 and 4 reversed	Template 9
D	Medium green print	4	Template 5 (page 87)

For rotary-cutting options, see the template patterns on the pages listed above.

Sewing

1. Sew the light green and red C pieces together in pairs, making four chevron units with the light green on the left and four with the light green on the right. Stitch in the direction of the arrow, stopping ¼" from both raw edges. Backstitch.

Make 4.   Make 4.

2. Sew the light green sides of the chevrons together in pairs. Stitch in the direction of the arrow, stopping ¼" from both raw edges. Backstitch. Make four.

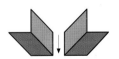 

Make 4.

3. Referring to "Set-in Seams" (page 10), add one ecru A square and two ecru B triangles to each chevron unit, stitching in the direction of the arrows.

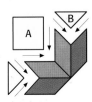

4. Sew a green D triangle to each chevron unit to complete the four corner units.

Make 4.

5. Sew an ecru A square to a medium green A square. Make four.

Make 4.

6. Sew the block into three vertical rows, using the completed corner units, the units from step 5, and the beige A square as shown. Join the vertical rows to complete the block.

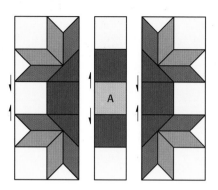

Devil's Claws

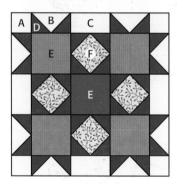

Finished size: 12"

Be sober, be watchful. Your adversary the devil prowls around like a roaring lion, seeking someone to devour. Resist him, firm in your faith, knowing that the same experience of suffering is required of your brotherhood throughout the world. And after you have suffered a little while, the God of all grace, who has called you to his eternal glory in Christ, will himself restore, establish, and strengthen you.

1 Peter 5:8–10

Cutting

PIECE	FABRIC	NUMBER TO CUT	SIZE
A	Ecru print	4 squares	2" x 2"
B	Ecru print	2 squares	4¼" x 4¼"; cut twice diagonally to yield 8 triangles
C	Ecru print	4 rectangles	2" x 3½"
D	Red print	16 squares	2⅜" x 2⅜"; cut once diagonally to yield 32 triangles
E	Tan print #1	4 squares	3½" x 3½"
	Tan print #2	1 square	3½" x 3½"
F	Light red print	4 squares	2⅝" x 2⅝"

Sewing

1. Sew a red D triangle to each short side of an ecru B triangle. Make eight.

Make 8.

2. Sew the remaining red D triangles to opposite sides of a light red F square, then to the remaining two sides as shown. Make four.

Make 4.

3. Sew the completed units together with the ecru A squares, the ecru C rectangles, the tan #1 E squares, and the tan #2 E square into five vertical rows as shown.

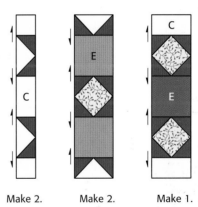

Make 2. Make 2. Make 1.

4. Join the rows to complete the block.

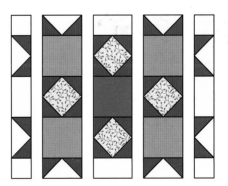

Double Cross

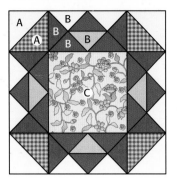

Finished size: 12"

So they took Jesus, and he went out, bearing his own cross, to the place called the place of a skull, which is called in Hebrew Golgotha. There they crucified him, and with him two others, one on either side, and Jesus between them.

John 19:17–18

Cutting

PIECE	FABRIC	NUMBER TO CUT	SIZE
A	Ecru print	2 squares	3⅞" x 3⅞"; cut once diagonally to yield 4 triangles
	Green check	2 squares	3⅞" x 3⅞"; cut once diagonally to yield 4 triangles
B	Tan print	1 square	4¼" x 4¼"; cut twice diagonally to yield 4 triangles
	Red print	3 squares	4¼" x 4¼"; cut twice diagonally to yield 12 triangles
	Green print	2 squares	4¼" x 4¼"; cut twice diagonally to yield 8 triangles
	Ecru print	2 squares	4¼" x 4¼"; cut twice diagonally to yield 8 triangles
C	Large-scale light red print	1 square	6½" x 6½"

Sewing

1. Sew an ecru A triangle to a green check A triangle. Make four.

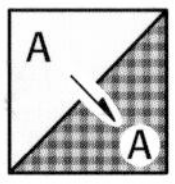

Make 4.

2. Sew a tan B triangle to a red B triangle; then sew two more red B triangles to this unit as shown. Make four.

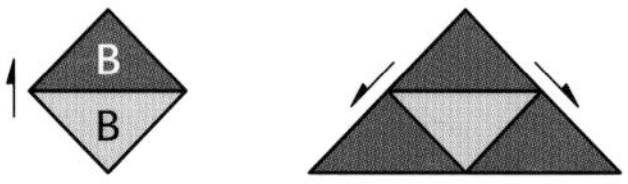

Make 4.

3. Sew a green B triangle to an ecru B triangle. Make four and four reversed.

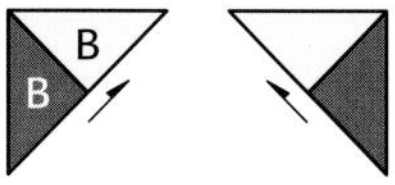

Make 4 of each.

4. Sew a unit from step 3 to each short side of a unit from step 2. Make four.

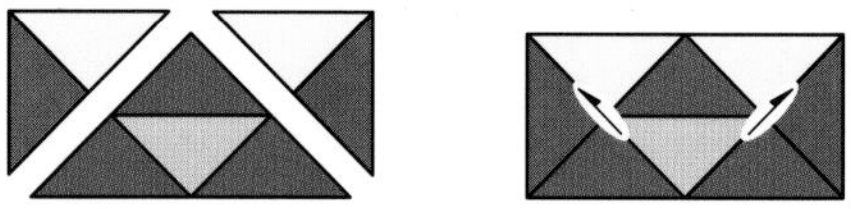

Make 4.

5. Sew a unit from step 1 to each end of a unit from step 4. Make two.

Make 2.

6. Arrange all the completed units into three vertical rows, adding the light red C square to the center row as shown. Sew the center row, then join the rows to complete the block.

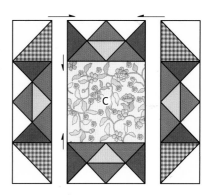

Dove in the Window

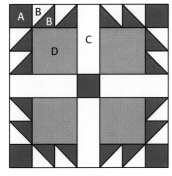

Finished size: 12"

Behold, I send you out as sheep in the midst of wolves; so be wise as serpents and innocent as doves.

Matthew 10:16

Cutting

PIECE	FABRIC	NUMBER TO CUT	SIZE
A	Brown print	5 squares	2¼" x 2¼"
B	Brown print	16	Template 10 (page 88)
	Ecru print	16	Template 10
C	Ecru print	4	Template 11 (page 88)
D	Tan print	4	Template 12 (page 88)

Sewing

1. Sew a brown B piece to an ecru B piece. Make 16.

Make 16.

2. Sew two units from step 1 together. Make four and four reversed.

Make 4 and 4 reversed.

3. Sew a brown A square to the right side of a reversed unit from step 2. Make four.

Make 4.

4. Sew a remaining unit from step 2 and a unit from step 3 to a tan D square as shown. Make four corner units.

Make 4.

5. Sew the completed corner units, the brown A square, and the ecru C rectangles together into three vertical rows as shown. Join the vertical rows together to complete the block.

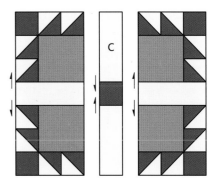

Garden of Eden

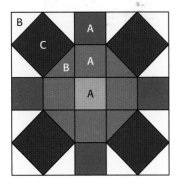

Finished size: 12"

And the Lord God planted a garden in Eden, in the east; and there he put the man whom he had formed. And out of the ground the Lord God made to grow every tree that is pleasant to the sight and good for food, the tree of life also in the midst of the garden, and the tree of the knowledge of good and evil.

Genesis 2:8–9

Cutting

PIECE	FABRIC	NUMBER TO CUT	SIZE
A	Brown print	4	Template 4 (page 87)
	Red print	4	Template 4
	Light green print	1	Template 4
B	Ecru print	12	Template 5 (page 87)
	Red print	4	Template 5
C	Dark green print	4	Template 13 (page 89)

For rotary-cutting options, see the template patterns on the pages listed above.

Sewing

1. Sew two ecru B triangles to opposite sides of a dark green C square. Make four.

Make 4.

2. Sew an ecru B triangle and a red B triangle to the remaining sides of a dark green C square as shown. Make four.

Make 4.

3. Sew a brown A square to a red A square. Make four.

Make 4.

4. Assemble all the completed units and the light green A square into three vertical rows as shown. Sew the rows together to complete the block.

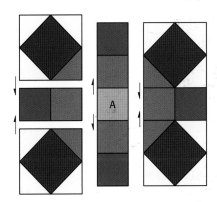

Garden Walk

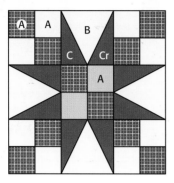

Finished size: 12"

I come to the garden alone,
While the dew is still on the roses;
And the voice I hear,
Falling on my ear,
The Son of God discloses.
And he walks with me, and He talks with me,
And he tells me I am His own;
And the joy we share as we tarry there,
None other has ever known.

From the hymn "In the Garden" by C. Austin Miles

Cutting

PIECE	FABRIC	NUMBER TO CUT	SIZE
A	Ecru print	1 strip	2½" x 21"
	Red plaid	1 strip	2½" x 21"
		2 squares	2½" x 2½"
	Tan print	2 squares	2½" x 2½"
B*	Ecru print	4	Template 14 (page 89)
C*	Green print	4 and 4 reversed	Template 15 (page 89)

If you prefer to paper piece the star-points unit, copy or trace the foundation pattern on page 92 onto paper. Make four foundation patterns. For the C pieces, cut four green print rectangles, 3¾" x 5¾"; layer them in pairs right sides together and cut once diagonally. Refer to "Paper Piecing" on page 11.

Sewing

1. Stitch the ecru print and red plaid strips, right sides together, along one long edge. Press toward the red strip. Cut the strip-pieced unit into eight 2½"-wide segments.

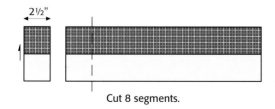

2½"

Cut 8 segments.

2. Sew the segments from step 1 together to make four-patch units as shown. Make four.

Make 4.

3. Sew a red plaid A square to a tan A square. Make two. Sew these units together to make a four-patch unit as shown.

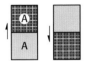

4. Sew a green C piece and a green C reversed piece to the long sides of an ecru B piece as shown. Or, paper piece the star point units using the foundation pattern on page 92, referring to "Paper Piecing" (page 11) as needed. Make four.

Make 4.

5. Using all the completed units, assemble three vertical rows as shown. Sew the rows together to complete the block.

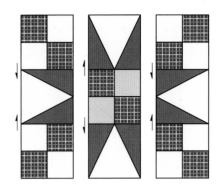

Golgotha

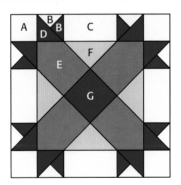

Finished size: 12"

So they took Jesus, and he went out, bearing his own cross, to the place called the place of a skull, which is called in Hebrew Golgotha.

John 19:17

Cutting

PIECE	FABRIC	NUMBER TO CUT	SIZE
A	Ecru print	4 squares	2½" x 2½"
B	Ecru print	2 squares	3¼" x 3¼"; cut twice diagonally to yield 8 triangles
	Red print	2 squares	3¼" x 3¼"; cut twice diagonally to yield 8 triangles
C	Ecru print	4 rectangles	2½" x 4½"
D	Red print	4 squares	2⅞" x 2⅞"; cut once diagonally to yield 8 triangles
E	Green print	4	Template 16 (page 89)
F	Tan print	1 square	5¼" x 5¼"; cut twice diagonally to yield 4 triangles
G	Red print	1	Template 17 (page 89)

Sewing

1. Sew two green E pieces to opposite sides of the red G square.

2. Sew two tan F triangles to opposite sides of a green E piece. Make two.

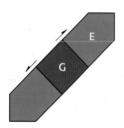

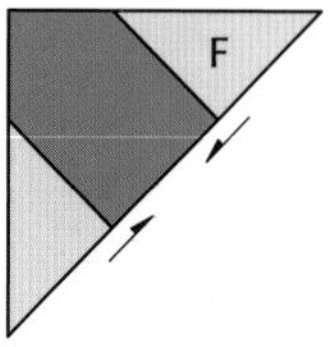

Make 2.

3. Stitch the units from step 2 together with the unit from step 1 as shown to complete the center unit.

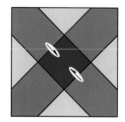

4. Sew a red B triangle to an ecru B triangle as shown. Make four and four reversed.

Make 4 of each.

5. Sew a unit from step 4 to a red D triangle as shown. Make four and four reversed.

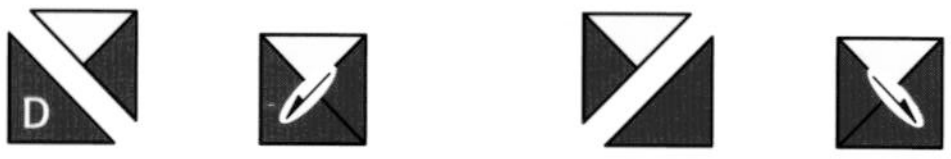

Make 4.   Make 4 reversed.

6. Sew the units from step 5 to opposite ends of each ecru C rectangle, paying careful attention to placement. Make four.

Make 4.

7. Sew an ecru A square to each end of two units from step 6. Make two.

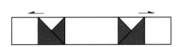

Make 2.

8. Sew all the completed units together in three vertical rows as shown. Join the rows to complete the block.

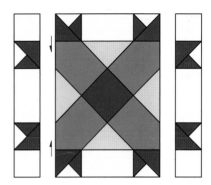

Heavenly Problems

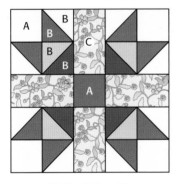

Finished size: 12"

Now war arose in heaven, Michael and his angels fighting against the dragon; and the dragon and his angels fought, but they were defeated and there was no longer any place for them in heaven. And the great dragon was thrown down, that ancient serpent, who is called the Devil and Satan, the deceiver of the whole world—he was thrown down to the earth, and his angels were thrown down with him.

Revelation 12:7–9

Cutting

PIECE	FABRIC	NUMBER TO CUT	SIZE
A	Ecru print	4	Template 4 (page 87)
	Red print	1	Template 4
B	Ecru print	8	Template 5 (page 87)
	Red print	8	Template 5
	Green print	4	Template 5
	Tan print	4	Template 5
C	Light red print	4	Template 6 (page 87)

For rotary-cutting options, see the template patterns on the pages listed above.

Sewing

1. Sew an ecru B triangle to a red B triangle. Make eight.

Make 8.

2. Sew a green B triangle to a tan B triangle. Make four.

Make 4.

3. Sew an ecru A square to a unit made in step 1. Make four.

Make 4.

4. Sew a unit made in step 1 to a unit made in step 2. Make four.

Make 4.

5. Join the completed units together to make four corner units as shown.

Make 4.

6. Using the completed corner units, the red A square, and the light red C rectangles, assemble the pieces into three vertical rows as shown. Sew the rows together to complete the block.

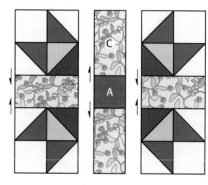

Heavenly Stars

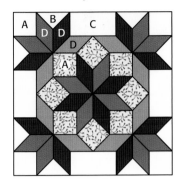

Finished size: 12"

I will multiply your descendants as the stars of heaven, and will give to your descendants all these lands; and by your descendants all the nations of the earth shall bless themselves: because Abraham obeyed my voice and kept my charge, my commandments, my statutes, and my laws.

Genesis 26:4–5

Note: This is one of the more challenging blocks in the book. You might want to gain experience with easier blocks before making this one.

Cutting

PIECE	FABRIC	NUMBER TO CUT	SIZE
A	Light red print	8 squares	2¼" x 2¼"
	Ecru print	4 squares	2¼" x 2¼"
B	Ecru print	2 squares	3¾" x 3¾"; cut twice diagonally to yield 8 triangles
C	Ecru print	4 rectangles	2¼" x 4"
D	Green print	12	Template 1 (page 87)
	Red print	12	Template 1
	Tan print	8	Template 1

Sewing

1. Sew four green and four red D pieces together in pairs, making four chevron units. Stitch in the direction of the arrow, stopping ¼" from both raw edges. Backstitch.

Make 4.

2. Sew the chevrons together to make the center star, stitching in the direction of the arrows and stopping ¼" from both raw edges. Backstitch. Press the seams open. Fan out the seams around the center point to reduce bulk.

3. Referring to "Set-in Seams" (page 10), add the light red A squares between the star points, stitching in the direction of the arrows. Begin and end stitching ¼" from the raw edges at both the inner corner and outer point as indicated by the dots in the square. Backstitch.

4. In the same manner, sew the tan D pieces to the light red squares, stitching from the outer dot to the point on each as indicated by the arrows.

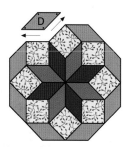

5. For the corner units, use the remaining green and red D pieces to sew sets of chevrons as shown. Make four and four reversed. Stitch as shown in step 1.

Make 4 of each.

6. Sew the chevron units together as shown. Make four.

Make 4.

7. Add an ecru A square and two ecru B triangles to each corner unit as shown, stitching in the direction of the arrows.

8. Stitch each corner unit to the center star unit. Begin and end stitching ¼" from the raw edges at both ends of the seam. Backstitch.

9. To complete the block, set in one ecru C rectangle at each side, stitching the long side to the block first and then the short sides. Stitch in the direction of the arrows.

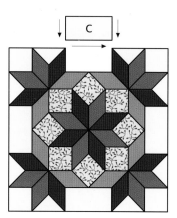

Hosanna

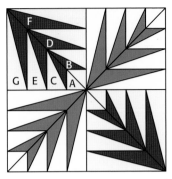

Finished size: 12"

And those who went before and those who followed cried out, "Hosanna! Blessed is he who comes in the name of the Lord! Blessed is the kingdom of our father David that is coming! Hosanna in the highest!"

Mark 11:9–10

Note: This block is designed for paper piecing. Cut fabric strips 2¼" wide and at least ¾" longer than the area to be covered. Use the chart below if you want to subcut the 2¼" strips before piecing the blocks.

Cutting

PIECE	FABRIC	NUMBER TO CUT	SIZE
A	Ecru print #1	4 rectangles	2¼" x 2½"
	Ecru print #2	4 rectangles	2¼" x 2½"
B	Green print #1	4 rectangles	2¼" x 4"
	Green print #2	4 rectangles	2¼" x 4"
C	Ecru print #1	4 rectangles	2¼" x 4¾"
	Ecru print #2	4 rectangles	2¼" x 4¾"
D	Green print #1	4 rectangles	2¼" x 5½"
	Green print #2	4 rectangles	2¼" x 5½"
E	Ecru print #1	4 rectangles	2¼" x 6"
	Ecru print #2	4 rectangles	2¼" x 6"
F	Green print #1	4 rectangles	2¼" x 7"
	Green print #2	4 rectangles	2¼" x 7"
G	Ecru print #1	4 rectangles	2¼" x 7¼"
	Ecru print #2	4 rectangles	2¼" x 7¼"

Sewing

1. Refer to "Paper Piecing" (page 11). Copy or trace the foundation patterns on page 93. Make four copies of both patterns and cut them out. You will have four sections and four sections reversed.

2. Place an ecru #1 A rectangle right side up on the foundation, making sure that the fabric extends past the ends of the foundation paper. Add a green #1 B rectangle, right sides together, and stitch on the drawn line.

3. Continue adding ecru #1 and green #1 strips until the whole section is covered.

4. Make two sections and two sections reversed from ecru #1 and green #1.

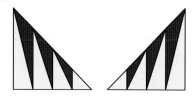

Make 2 of each.

5. Trim the fabric extending around the edge of the foundation paper so that there is a ¼" seam allowance around each section. Pin two sections together. Baste the sections to make one quarter of the block. Check that the pieces line up exactly; then sew. Make two sections.

Make 2.

6. Repeat steps 1–5, using ecru #2 and green #2. Make two.

Make 2.

7. Sew the quarter blocks together into two vertical rows, paying careful attention to the position of each A piece. Join the vertical rows to complete the block.

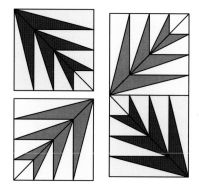

8. Carefully remove the foundation paper.

Job's Troubles

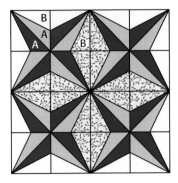

Finished size: 12"

Now when Job's three friends heard of all this evil that had come upon him, they came each from his own place.... They made an appointment together to come to condole with him and comfort him. And when they saw him from afar, they did not recognize him; and they raised their voices and wept; and they rent their robes and sprinkled dust upon their heads toward heaven. And they sat with him on the ground seven days and seven nights, and no one spoke a word to him, for they saw that his suffering was very great.

Job 2:11–13

Note: This block is designed for paper piecing. Cut the red and gold fabric strips 1¾" wide and at least ¾" longer than the area to be covered. Cut the ecru and light red print strips 2¼" wide. Use the chart below if you wish to subcut the strips before piecing the block.

Cutting

PIECE	FABRIC	NUMBER TO CUT	SIZE
A	Red print	16 rectangles	1¾" x 5½"
	Gold print	16 rectangles	1¾" x 5½"
B	Ecru print	16 rectangles	2¼" x 4½"
	Light red print	16 rectangles	2¼" x 4½"

Sewing

1. Refer to "Paper Piecing" (page 11). Copy or trace the foundation pattern on page 92 onto paper. Make 16 copies of the pattern and cut them out.

2. Start piecing with red and gold A rectangles, placing them right sides together along the diagonal center line. Make sure the fabric extends beyond the edge of the paper. Stitch on the diagonal line. Open out and press as shown.

3. Next add the ecru and light red B pieces. Pay careful attention to the placement of these strips. Make four of each variation.

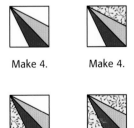

Make 4.   Make 4.

Make 4.   Make 4.

4. Trim the excess fabric so that there is ¼" seam allowance around each section.

5. Arrange four sections as shown. Pin two sections together and baste. Check that the points match. Sew the two sections and then the two halves together to make one quarter of the block. Repeat to make four units.

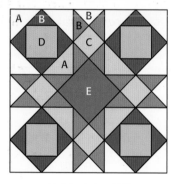

Make 4.

6. Baste and then sew the four units together to complete the block as shown.

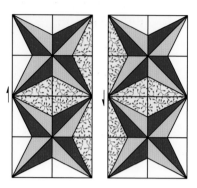

7. Carefully remove the foundation paper.

Joseph's Coat

Finished size: 12"

Now Israel loved Joseph more than all his children, because he was the son of his old age: and he made him a coat of many colours.

Genesis 37:3

Cutting

PIECE	FABRIC	NUMBER TO CUT	SIZE
A	Ecru print	12	Template 5 (page 87)
	Beige print	4	Template 5
B	Ecru print	4	Template 8 (page 88)
	Red print	16	Template 8
	Green print	16	Template 8
C	Beige print	4	Template 18 (page 90)
D	Tan print	4	Template 4 (page 87)
E	Brown print	1	Template 13 (page 89)

For rotary-cutting options, see the template patterns on the pages listed above.

Sewing

1. Sew a red B triangle to each short side of a beige A triangle. Make four.

Make 4.

2. Sew a beige C square to each end of two units from step 1. Make two.

Make 2.

3. Sew the units from step 1, the units from step 2, and the brown E square together as shown to make the center unit.

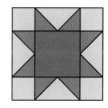

4. Sew two green B triangles to opposite sides of a tan D square. Repeat for the remaining sides of the square. Make four, one for each corner of the block.

Make 4.

5. Sew three ecru A triangles to three sides of a unit from step 4 as shown. Make four corner units.

Make 4.

6. Add two red B triangles to opposite sides of a corner unit. Make four.

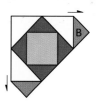

Make 4.

7. Sew two ecru B triangles to opposite sides of a corner unit as shown. Make two.

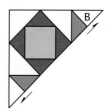

Make 2.

8. Join the two remaining units from step 6 to the center unit as shown. Then sew the units from step 7 to the center unit to complete the block.

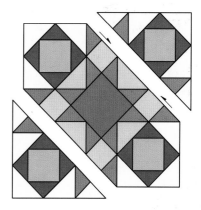

King David's Crown

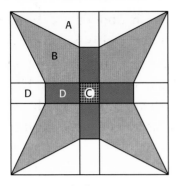

Finished size: 12"

So all the elders of Israel came to the king at Hebron; and King David made a covenant with them at Hebron before the Lord, and they anointed David King over Israel. David was thirty years old when he began to reign, and he reigned forty years.

2 Samuel 5:3–4

Note: Part of this block is designed for paper piecing. Cut fabric pieces for A and B at least ¾" wider and longer than the area to be covered. Use the chart below to cut the fabric pieces for the block.

Cutting

PIECE	FABRIC	NUMBER TO CUT	SIZE
A	Ecru print	8 rectangles	3½" x 7¼"
B	Tan print	4 rectangles	4¾" x 8¾"
C	Brown print	1 square	2" x 2"
D	Brown print	4 rectangles	2" x 3⅛"
	Ecru print	4 rectangles	2" x 3⅛"

Sewing

1. Refer to "Paper Piecing" (page 11). Copy or trace the foundation pattern on page 94 onto paper. Make four copies of the pattern and cut them out. Paper piece the four corner units, beginning with the tan B rectangle in each center. Trim the excess fabric so that there is a ¼" seam allowance around each corner unit.

Make 4.

2. Sew together the brown and ecru D rectangles. Make four.

Make 4.

3. Join together the brown C square with two units from step 2.

4. Assemble all the pieced units to make three vertical rows as shown. Join the three rows to complete the block.

5. Carefully remove the foundation papers.

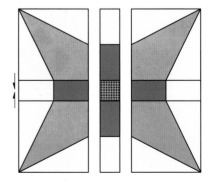

King's Crown

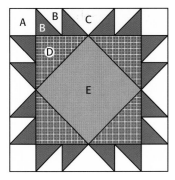

Finished size: 12"

And Haman said to the king, "For the man whom the king delights to honor, let royal robes be brought, which the king has worn, and the horse which the king has ridden, and on whose head a royal crown is set; and let the robes and the horse be handed over to one of the king's most noble princes; let him array the man whom the king delights to honor, and let him conduct the man on horseback through the open square of the city."

Esther 6:7–9

Cutting

PIECE	FABRIC	NUMBER TO CUT	SIZE
A	Ecru print	4 squares	2½" x 2½"
B	Ecru print	4 squares	2⅞" x 2⅞"; cut once diagonally to yield 8 triangles
	Brown print	8 squares	2⅞" x 2⅞"; cut once diagonally to yield 16 triangles
C	Ecru print	1 square	5¼" x 5¼"; cut twice diagonally to yield 4 triangles
D	Red plaid	2 squares	4⅞" x 4⅞"; cut once diagonally to yield 4 triangles
E	Tan print	1 square	6⅛" x 6⅛"

Sewing

1. Sew two red plaid D triangles to opposite sides of the tan E square. Sew the remaining two red plaid D triangles to the remaining two sides of the square as shown to complete the center unit.

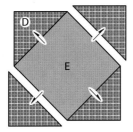

2. Sew a brown B triangle to an ecru B triangle. Make eight.

Make 8.

3. Sew a brown B triangle to each short side of an ecru C triangle as shown. Make four.

Make 4.

4. Sew a unit from step 2 to each end of a unit from step 3. Make four.

Make 4.

5. Sew an ecru A square to each end of a unit from step 4. Make two.

Make 2.

6. Sew all the completed units together to make three vertical rows as shown at right. Join the vertical rows to complete the block.

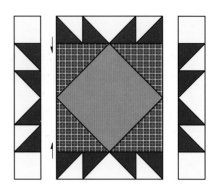

Road to Damascus

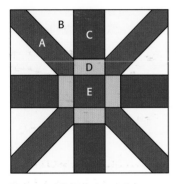

Finished size: 12"

But Saul, still breathing threats and murder against the disciples of the Lord, went to the high priest and asked him for letters to the synagogues at Damascus, so that if he found any belonging to the Way, men or women, he might bring them bound to Jerusalem. Now as he journeyed he approached Damascus, and suddenly a light from heaven flashed about him. And he fell to the ground and heard a voice saying to him, "Saul, Saul, why do you persecute me?" And he said, "Who are you, Lord?" And he said, "I am Jesus, whom you are persecuting; but rise and enter the city, and you will be told what you are to do."

Acts 9:1–6

Cutting

PIECE	FABRIC	NUMBER TO CUT	SIZE
A	Green print	4	Template 19 (page 90)
B	Ecru print	4 squares	4½" x 4½"; cut once diagonally to yield 8 triangles
C	Red print	4 rectangles	2⅞" x 4⅛"
D	Gold print	4	Template 20 (page 90)
E	Red print	1 square	2⅞" x 2⅞"

Sewing

1. Sew an ecru B triangle to each long side of a green A piece as shown. Make four.

Make 4.

2. Sew a red C rectangle to a gold D piece. Make four.

Make 4.

3. Assemble the completed units and the red E square into three vertical rows as shown. Join the rows to complete the block.

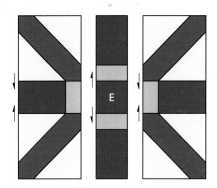

Road to Paradise

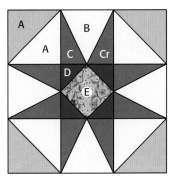

Finished size: 12"

And I saw the holy city, new Jerusalem, coming down out of heaven from God, prepared as a bride adorned for her husband; and I heard a loud voice from the throne saying, "Behold, the dwelling of God is with men. He will dwell with them, and they shall be his people, and God himself will be with them; he will wipe away every tear from their eyes, and death shall be no more, neither shall there be mourning nor crying nor pain any more, for the former things have passed away."

Revelation 21:2–4

Cutting

PIECE	FABRIC	NUMBER TO CUT	SIZE
A	Tan print	2 squares	4⅞" x 4⅞"; cut once diagonally to yield 4 triangles
	Ecru print	2 squares	4⅞" x 4⅞"; cut once diagonally to yield 4 triangles
B*	Ecru print	4	Template 14 (page 89)
C*	Brown print	4 and 4 reversed	Template 15 (page 89)
D	Red print	2 squares	2⅞" x 2⅞"; cut once diagonally to yield 4 triangles
E	Tan multicolored print	1	Template 21 (page 90)

If you prefer to paper piece the star-point units, copy or trace the foundation pattern on page 92 onto paper. Make four foundation patterns. For the C pieces, cut four rectangles from the brown print, 3¾" x 5¾"; layer them in pairs right sides together and cut once diagonally. Refer to "Paper Piecing" on page 11.

Sewing

1. Sew a tan A triangle to an ecru A triangle. Make four.

Make 4.

2. Sew a brown C piece and a brown C reversed piece to opposite sides of an ecru B piece as shown. Or, paper piece the star point units using the foundation pattern on page 92, referring to "Paper Piecing" (page 11) as needed. Make four.

Make 4.

3. Sew two red D triangles to opposite sides of the tan E square. Repeat on the remaining sides to complete the center unit.

4. Sew all the completed units into three vertical rows as shown. Sew the rows together to complete the block.

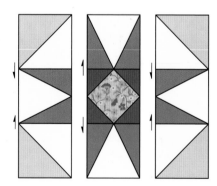

Robbing Peter to Pay Paul

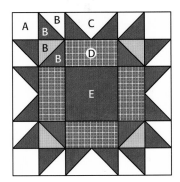

Finished size: 12"

He said to them, "But who do you say that I am?" Simon Peter replied, "You are the Christ, the Son of the living God." And Jesus answered him, "Blessed are you, Simon Bar-Jona! For flesh and blood has not revealed this to you, but my Father who is in heaven. And I tell you, you are Peter, and on this rock I will build my church, and the powers of death shall not prevail against it."

Matthew 16:15–18

And God did extraordinary miracles by the hands of Paul, so that handkerchiefs or aprons were carried away from his body to the sick, and diseases left them and the evil spirits came out of them.

Acts 19:11–12

Cutting

PIECE	FABRIC	NUMBER TO CUT	SIZE
A	Ecru print	4 squares	2½" x 2½"
B	Ecru print	4 squares	2⅞" x 2⅞"; cut once diagonally to yield 8 triangles
	Tan print	2 squares	2⅞" x 2⅞"; cut once diagonally to yield 4 triangles
	Green print	8 squares	2⅞" x 2⅞"; cut once diagonally to yield 16 triangles
	Red print	2 squares	2⅞" x 2⅞"; cut once diagonally to yield 4 triangles
C	Ecru print	1 square	5¼" x 5¼"; cut twice diagonally to yield 4 triangles
D	Red plaid	4 rectangles	2½" x 4½"
E	Green print	1 square	4½" x 4½"

Sewing

1. Sew two red plaid D rectangles to opposite sides of the green E square.

2. Sew a tan B triangle to a red B triangle. Make four.

Make 4.

3. Sew a unit from step 2 to each end of the remaining red plaid D rectangles. Make two.

Make 2.

4. Sew the units from step 3 to opposite sides of the unit from step 1 to complete the center unit.

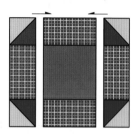

5. Sew a green B triangle to each short side of an ecru C triangle. Make four.

Make 4.

6. Sew a green B triangle to an ecru B triangle. Make eight.

Make 8.

7. Sew a unit from step 6 to each end of a unit from step 5. Make four.

Make 4.

8. Sew an ecru A square to each end of two units from step 7.

Make 2.

9. Assemble all the pieced units as shown to complete the block.

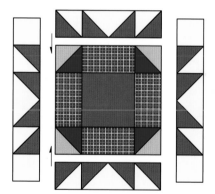

Solomon's Puzzle

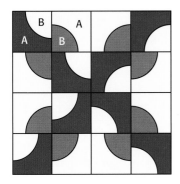

Finished size: 12"

Then the king said, "The one says, 'This is my son that is alive, and your son is dead'; and the other says, 'No; but your son is dead, and my son is the living one.'" And the king said, "Bring me a sword." So a sword was brought before the king. And the king said, "Divide the living child in two, and give half to the one, and half to the other." Then the woman whose son was alive said to the king, because her heart yearned for her son, "Oh, my lord, give her the living child, and by no means slay it". . . Then the king answered and said, "Give the living child to the first woman, and by no means slay it; she is its mother."

1 Kings 3:23–27

Cutting

PIECE	FABRIC	NUMBER TO CUT	SIZE
A	Red print	8 squares	3½" x 3½"
	Ecru print	8 squares	3½" x 3½"

Preparing the Appliqués

1. Using template 22 (page 90), trace 16 shapes onto freezer paper. Cut out the shapes right on the marked line.

2. Press eight paper shapes to the wrong side of the green fabric and press eight shapes to the wrong side of the ecru fabric.

3. Cut out all the shapes leaving ¼" seam allowances around the edges of the freezer paper.

Appliqué and Sewing

1. Referring to "Freezer-Paper Appliqué" (page 13), glue the curved seam allowances on all the appliqué shapes and turn under along the edge of the freezer paper.

2. Place the green appliqué shapes onto the ecru A squares. Glue in place as shown and stitch along the curved edge with an invisible appliqué stitch. Make eight.

Make 8.

3. Place the ecru appliqué shapes onto the red A squares and repeat step 2. Make eight.

Make 8.

4. Lay out the units referring to the block diagram for color placement and stitch the units together in four vertical rows as shown. Join the rows to complete the block.

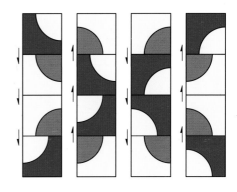

Solomon's Star

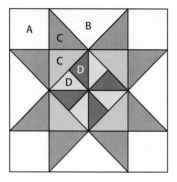

Finished size: 12"

And God gave Solomon wisdom and understanding beyond measure, and largeness of mind like the sand on the seashore, so that Solomon's wisdom surpassed the wisdom of all the people of the east, and all the wisdom of Egypt.

1 Kings 4:29–30

Cutting

PIECE	FABRIC	NUMBER TO CUT	SIZE
A	Ecru print	4 squares	3½" x 3½"
B	Ecru print	1 square	7¼" x 7¼"; cut twice diagonally to yield 4 triangles
C	Tan print	2 squares	3⅞" x 3⅞"; cut once diagonally to yield 4 triangles
	Light brown print	4 squares	3⅞" x 3⅞"; cut once diagonally to yield 8 triangles
D	Green print	2 squares	3" x 3"; cut once diagonally to yield 4 triangles
	Beige print	2 squares	3" x 3"; cut once diagonally to yield 4 triangles

Sewing

1. Sew a green D triangle to a beige D triangle. Make four.

Make 4.

2. Join the units from step 1 to make a pinwheel unit.

3. Sew two tan C triangles to opposite sides of the pinwheel. Repeat with the remaining two tan C triangles.

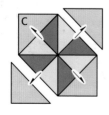

4. Sew a light brown C triangle to each short side of an ecru B triangle. Make four.

Make 4.

5. Sew all the completed units and the ecru A squares together into three vertical rows as shown. Join the rows to complete the block.

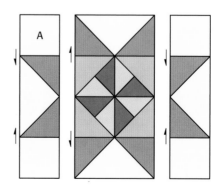

Star and Cross

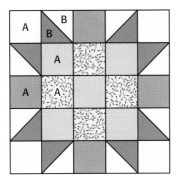

Finished size: 12"

Near the Cross, a trembling soul,
Love and mercy found me;
There the Bright and Morning Star
Sheds its beams around me.

From the hymn "Near the Cross"
by Fanny J. Crosby and William H. Doane

Cutting

PIECE	FABRIC	NUMBER TO CUT	SIZE
A	Ecru print	4	Template 4 (page 87)
	Tan print	5	Template 4
	Light brown print	4	Template 4
	Light red print	4	Template 4
B	Ecru print	8	Template 5 (page 87)
	Red print	8	Template 5

For rotary-cutting options, see the template patterns on the pages listed above.

Sewing

1. Sew an ecru B triangle to a red B triangle. Make eight.

Make 8.

2. Join the units from step 1 with the ecru, tan, light brown, and light red A squares as shown to make five vertical rows. Sew the rows together to complete the block.

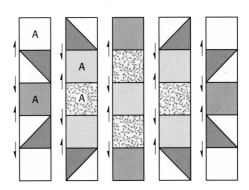

Star-Crossed Christmas

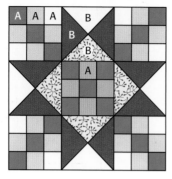

Finished size: 12"

O little town of Bethlehem,
How still we see thee lie!
Above thy deep and dreamless sleep
The silent stars go by
Yet in thy dark street shineth
The everlasting Light;
The hopes and fears of all the years
Are met in thee tonight.

From the hymn "O Little Town of Bethlehem"
by Phillips Brooks and Lewis H. Redner

Cutting

PIECE	FABRIC	NUMBER TO CUT	SIZE
A*	Green print	17	Template 23 (page 90)
	Ecru print	8	Template 23
	Tan print	4	Template 23
	Beige print	16	Template 23
B	Ecru print	1 square	5¼" x 5¼"; cut twice diagonally to yield 4 triangles
	Red print	2 squares	5¼" x 5¼"; cut twice diagonally to yield 8 triangles
	Light red print	1 square	5¼" x 5¼"; cut twice diagonally to yield 4 triangles

*If you wish to rotary cut the A squares, the measurement is 1¾" plus ⅟₁₆".

Sewing

1. Sew a red B triangle to an ecru B triangle. Make four.

Make 4.

2. Sew a red B triangle to a light red B triangle. Make four.

Make 4.

3. Sew the units from steps 1 and 2 together as shown. Make four.

Make 4.

4. Sew the center nine-patch unit by joining five green A pieces with four tan A pieces as shown.

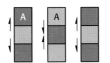

5. Sew a corner nine-patch unit by joining three green A pieces, four beige A pieces, and two ecru A pieces as shown. Make four.

Make 4.

6. Sew all the units together to make three vertical rows as shown. Join the rows together to complete the block.

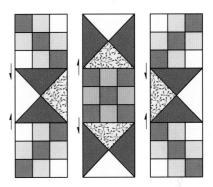

Star of the Magi

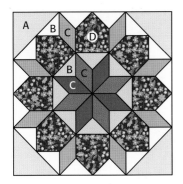

Finished size: 12"

Now when Jesus was born in Bethlehem of Judea in the days of Herod the king, behold, wise men from the East came to Jerusalem, saying, "Where is he who has been born king of the Jews? For we have seen his star in the East, and have come to worship him."

Matthew 2:1–2

 Note: This is one of the more challenging blocks in the book. You might want to gain experience with easier blocks before making this one.

Cutting

PIECE	FABRIC	NUMBER TO CUT	SIZE
A	Tan print	2 squares	4⅜" x 4⅜"; cut once diagonally to yield 4 triangles
B	Ecru print	4 squares	3¾" x 3¾"; cut twice diagonally to yield 16 triangles
	Beige print	2 squares	3¾" x 3¾"; cut twice diagonally to yield 8 triangles
C	Medium green print	8	Template 1 (page 87)
	Dark green print	4	Template 1
	Red print	4	Template 1
D	Green multicolored print	8	Template 24 (page 90)

Sewing

1. To make the center star, make four chevron units using the red and dark green C pieces. Stitch in the direction of the arrow, beginning and ending the stitching ¼" from both raw edges. Backstitch. Press the seams open.

Make 4.

2. Sew the chevrons together into star points, stitching in the direction of the arrows and stopping ¼" from both raw edges. Backstitch. Press the seams open. Fan out the seams around the center point to reduce bulk.

3. Referring to "Set-in Seams" (page 10), sew a beige B triangle between each set of star points. Stitch in the direction of the arrows.

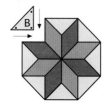

4. Stitch eight green multicolored D pieces to the star unit as shown. Stop stitching ¼" from both raw edges. Backstitch.

5. Stitch the medium green C diamonds between the D pieces as shown. Stop stitching ¼" from both raw edges. Backstitch.

6. Using set-in seams, insert an ecru B triangle between each set of points, stitching in the direction of the arrows.

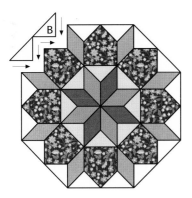

7. Add a tan A triangle to each corner to complete the block.

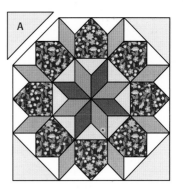

Storm at Sea

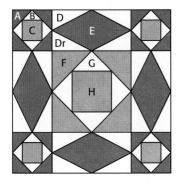

Finished size: 12"

And behold, there arose a great storm on the sea, so that the boat was being swamped by the waves; but he was asleep. And they went and woke him, saying, "Save us, Lord; we are perishing." And he said to them, "Why are you afraid, O men of little faith?" Then he rose and rebuked the winds and the sea; and there was a great calm. And the men marveled, saying, "What sort of man is this, that even winds and sea obey him?"

Matthew 8:24–27

Cutting

PIECE	FABRIC	NUMBER TO CUT	SIZE
A	Red print	8 squares	2⅜" x 2⅜"; cut once diagonally to yield 16 triangles
B	Ecru print	4 squares	2¾" x 2¾"; cut twice diagonally to yield 16 triangles
C	Tan print	4 squares	2" x 2"
D*	Ecru print	8 and 8 reversed	Template 25 (page 91)
E*	Red print	4	Template 26 (page 91)
F	Tan print	2 squares	3⅞" x 3⅞"; cut once diagonally to yield 4 triangles
G	Ecru print	2 squares	3" x 3"; cut once diagonally to yield 4 triangles
H	Tan print	1 square	3½" x 3½"

If you prefer to paper piece the D/E units, copy or trace the foundation pattern on page 91 onto paper. Make four foundation patterns. For the D pieces, cut 16 rectangles, 2½" x 4½", from the ecru print. Use template 26 as a guide to cut piece E. Refer to "Paper Piecing" on page 11.

Sewing

1. Sew two ecru G triangles to opposite sides of the tan H square. Repeat on the remaining sides of the unit.

Glad Tidings

Press the seams to the outside so that you can see exactly where to stitch the next pieces to maintain the points of the square.

2. Sew two tan F triangles to opposite sides of the unit from step 1. Repeat on the remaining sides to complete the center unit.

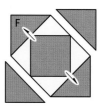

3. Sew two ecru D pieces to opposite sides of a red E piece, carefully matching the seam intersections. Sew two ecru D reversed pieces to the remaining two sides to complete the unit. Be sure to mark the dots on both the E and D pieces and match them up by pinning carefully before you sew. Or, paper piece the D/E units using the foundation pattern on page 91, referring to "Paper Piecing" (page 11) as needed. Make four.

Make 4.

4. Sew two ecru B triangles to opposite sides of a tan C square. Repeat on the remaining two sides. Make four.

5. Sew two red A triangles to opposite sides of the unit from step 4. Repeat on the remaining two sides to complete the corner unit. Make four.

Make 4.

6. Sew all the completed units together to make three vertical rows as shown. Join the vertical rows to complete the block.

Temple Court

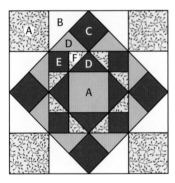

Finished size: 12"

Now his parents went to Jerusalem every year at the feast of the Passover. And when he was twelve years old, they went up according to custom; and when the feast was ended, as they were returning, the boy Jesus stayed behind in Jerusalem . . . After three days they found him in the temple, sitting among the teachers, listening to them and asking them questions; and all who heard him were amazed at his understanding and his answers.

Luke 2:41–43, 46–47

Cutting

PIECE	FABRIC	NUMBER TO CUT	SIZE
A	Gold print	1 square	3½" x 3½"
	Light red print	4 squares	3½" x 3½"
B	Ecru print	4 squares	3⅞" x 3⅞"; cut once diagonally to yield 8 triangles
C	Red print	4 squares	2⅝" x 2⅝"
D	Red print	1 square	4¼" x 4¼"; cut twice diagonally to yield 4 triangles
	Gold print	2 squares	4¼" x 4¼"; cut twice diagonally to yield 8 triangles
E	Red print	4 squares	2" x 2"
F	Light red print	4 squares	2⅜" x 2⅜"; cut once diagonally to yield 8 triangles

Sewing

1. Sew two red D triangles to opposite sides of the gold A square. Repeat on the remaining two sides.

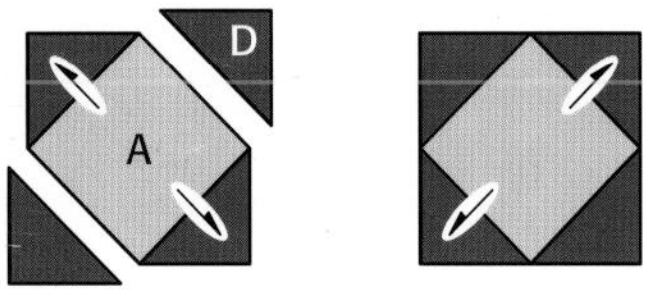

2. Sew two light red F triangles to adjoining sides of a red E square as shown. Make four.

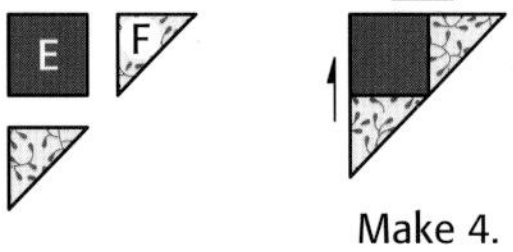

Make 4.

3. Sew two units from step 2 to opposite sides of the unit from step 1. Repeat on the remaining two sides.

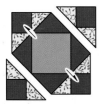

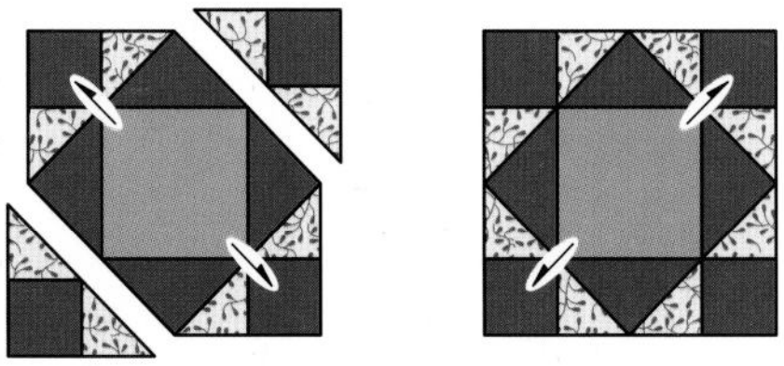

4. Sew two gold D triangles to adjoining sides of a red C square as shown. Make four.

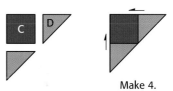

Make 4.

5. Sew an ecru B triangle to each short side of the unit from step 4. Make four.

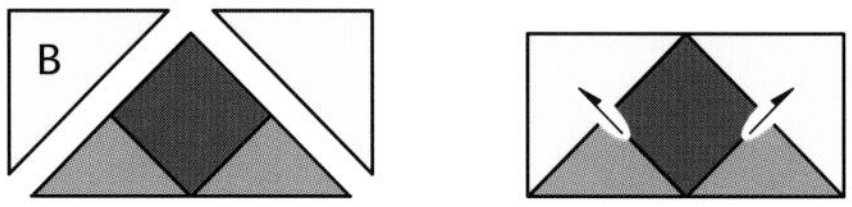

Make 4.

6. Sew all the completed units and the light red A squares together to make three vertical rows as shown. Join the vertical rows together to complete the block.

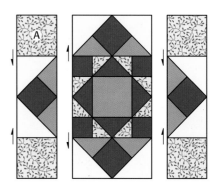

Wedding Ring

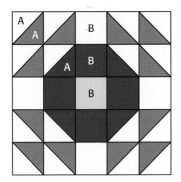

Finished size: 12"

He answered, "Have you not read that he who made them from the beginning made them male and female, and said 'For this reason a man shall leave his father and mother and be joined to his wife, and the two shall become one flesh'? So they are no longer two but one. What therefore God has joined together, let not man put asunder."

Matthew 19:4–6

Note: This block is also called Crown and Thorns.

Cutting

PIECE	FABRIC	NUMBER TO CUT	SIZE
A	Ecru print	16	Template 5 (page 87)
	Red print	4	Template 5
	Green print	12	Template 5
B	Ecru print	4	Template 4 (page 87)
	Tan print	1	Template 4
	Red print	4	Template 4

For rotary-cutting options, see the template patterns on the pages listed above.

Sewing

1. Sew an ecru A triangle to a green A triangle. Make 12.

Make 12.

2. Sew an ecru A triangle to a red A triangle. Make four.

Make 4.

3. Sew all the completed units and the ecru, tan, and red B squares into five vertical rows as shown. Join the vertical rows to complete the block.

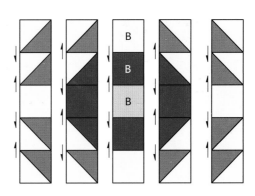

Whither Thou Goest

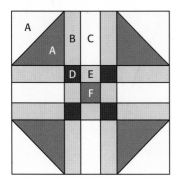

Finished size: 12"

But Ruth said, "Intreat me not to leave thee, or to return from following after thee; for whither thou goest, I will go; and where thou lodgest, I will lodge: thy people shall be my people, and thy God my God: Where thou diest, will I die, and there will I be buried: the Lord do so to me, and more also, if ought but death part thee and me."

Ruth 1:16–17

Cutting

PIECE	FABRIC	NUMBER TO CUT	SIZE
A	Ecru print	2 squares	4⅞" x 4⅞"; cut once diagonally to yield 4 triangles
	Red print	2 squares	4⅞" x 4⅞"; cut once diagonally to yield 4 triangles
B	Tan print	8 rectangles	1¾" x 4½"
C	Ecru print	4 rectangles	2" x 4½"
D	Green print	4 squares	1¾" x 1¾"
E	Tan print	4 rectangles	1¾" x 2"
F	Red print	1 square	2" x 2"

Sewing

1. Sew an ecru A triangle to a red A triangle. Make four.

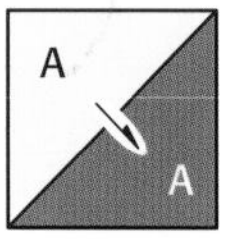

Make 4.

2. Sew two tan B rectangles to opposite sides of an ecru C rectangle. Make four.

Make 4.

3. Sew two D squares to opposite sides of a tan E rectangle. Make two. Sew two tan E rectangles to opposite sides of a red F square. Join these units together as shown to complete the center unit.

Make 2.

4. Join all the units together to make three vertical rows as shown. Join the vertical rows to complete the block.

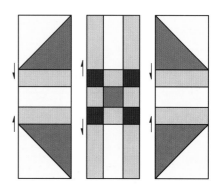

THIRTY-BLOCK SAMPLER: Block-to-Block Setting

Made by Rosemary Makhan. Machine quilted by Sue Patten.

Quilt size: 79½" x 91½" • Finished block: 12"

Making this quilt will provide many opportunities not only for creative expression but for practicing and perfecting a wide variety of piecing techniques and skills. I used antique sampler quilts from the late 1800s as inspiration for this setting. Choose 30 of the 32 blocks in the block gallery. Collect fat eighths and fat quarters in the colors of your choice. I used 8 to 10 different fabrics in each of my chosen colors: red, green, tan, beige, and ecru. These fabrics can be repeated in different combinations in the blocks. When you're finished, you will be very proud to have made such a meaningful and beautiful quilt.

Materials

3⅞ yards of large focal print for borders and binding

14 to 16 fat eighths and 22 to 26 fat quarters in 8 to 10 different reds, greens, tans, beiges, and ecrus for blocks and block backgrounds

8 yards* of fabric for backing and hanging sleeve (or 3 yards of 110"-wide fabric)

84" x 96" piece of batting

If your fabric is at least 42" wide after prewashing, 6 yards will be enough.

Cutting

PIECE	FABRIC	NUMBER TO CUT	SIZE
Top and bottom borders	Focal print	2 strips	10¼" x 84", from the lengthwise grain
Side borders	Focal print	2 strips	10¼" x 96", from the lengthwise grain
Binding	Focal print	10 strips	2¼" x 42", from the crosswise grain

Sewing

1. Stitch 30 blocks of your choice from the block gallery.

2. Arrange the blocks in rows of five across and six down so that the colors and patterns are balanced and pleasing.

◇

Glad Tidings

It is easier to sew the blocks together if the blocks placed next to each other have different grids—then the only seams that have to be matched up are the ones at the corners of each block.

3. Sew the blocks together into five vertical rows, pressing the joining seams in opposite directions from row to row. Join the rows.

4. Add the borders, referring to "Mitered Borders" (page 15).

Finishing the Quilt

Refer to "Finishing" (pages 16–18) for details on the following steps.

1. Prepare the backing and layer the quilt top, batting, and backing. Baste.

2. Quilt by hand or machine as desired and bind the quilt.

3. Make and add a hanging sleeve and label.

TWELVE-BLOCK SAMPLER:
Blocks Set On Point

Made by Rosemary Makhan. Machine quilted by Carol Cunningham.

Quilt size: 75" x 92" • Finished block: 12"

Here's a chance to feature a beautiful focal fabric (or two) and make 12 of your favorite blocks to coordinate with it. This wonderful floral chintz fabric provides an ideal backdrop for the 12 blocks. Collect fat eighths and fat quarters in colors that coordinate with the featured fabric. I used eight or more fabrics in different values of red, green, and ecru and four or more fabrics in different values of golden tan and light brown. This quilt is also a great opportunity to use up scraps in your fabric stash. The setting squares and border will tie all the colors together.

Materials

3 yards* of large floral print for outer border (can be the same as the alternate blocks and setting triangles)

2 yards* of large floral print for alternate blocks and setting triangles (side and corner)

6 to 8 fat eighths and 10 to 12 fat quarters in red, green, golden tan, light brown, and ecru

⅝ yard of red tone-on-tone for inner border

6¼ yards of fabric for backing and hanging sleeve

¾ yard of fabric for binding

79" x 96" piece of batting

Purchase an additional yard if you wish to center the focal fabric print design in the alternate blocks or if you wish to miter each corner at a specific place in the print.

Cutting

PIECE	FABRIC	NUMBER TO CUT	SIZE
Alternate blocks	Large floral print	6 squares	12½" x 12½"
Side setting triangles	Large floral print	3 squares	18¼" x 18¼"; cut twice diagonally to yield 12 triangles. You will use 10.
Corner setting triangles	Large floral print	2 squares	9⅜" x 9⅜"; cut once diagonally to yield 4 triangles
Inner borders	Red tone-on-tone	8 strips	2½" x 42"
Top and bottom borders*	Large floral print	2 strips	10½" x 80", from the lengthwise grain
Side borders*	Large floral print	2 strips	10½" x 97", from the lengthwise grain
Binding	Binding fabric	9 strips	2¼" x 42"

If your fabric is less than 42" wide, divide the fabric width by four and cut the borders as wide as possible.

Sewing

1. Make 12 blocks of your choice from the block gallery.

2. Sew the completed blocks and the alternate large floral print blocks together in diagonal rows as shown. Add the side and corner setting triangles as you sew each row. Press the seams away from the pieced blocks.

3. Join the diagonal rows, matching the seam lines as you stitch.

4. Sew the inner border strips together in groups of two and press the seams open. Sew the inner borders to the quilt top, mitering the corners. Refer to "Mitered Borders" (page 15).

5. Add the outer borders, mitering the corners.

Finishing the Quilt

Refer to "Finishing" (pages 16–18) for details on the following steps.

1. Prepare the backing and layer the quilt top, batting, and backing. Baste.

2. Quilt by hand or machine as desired and bind the quilt.

3. Make and add a hanging sleeve and label.

STAIRWAY TO HEAVEN: Alternate-Block Setting

Made and quilted by Corry Smit.

Quilt size: 87" x 104" • Finished block: 12"

I love the way the alternate block, Stairway to Heaven, creates a chain of squares around the sampler blocks. Corry used a beautiful bright focal fabric and a heavenly theme in the blocks and setting triangles. She chose medium blue, dark blue, turquoise, gold, and orange fabrics for the Biblical blocks and used at least four different fabrics in each of her color choices. These fabrics were repeated in different combinations in the blocks.

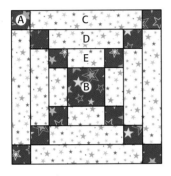

Stairway to Heaven

Materials

3⅜ yards of coordinating print for outer border

3¼ yards of focal print for blocks, alternate blocks, and setting triangles*

2¾ yards of light background print for alternate blocks

1⅝ yards of contrasting print for inner border and blocks

1 yard of light blue background print for blocks

6 to 8 fat eighths and 10 to 12 fat quarters in the colors of your choice for blocks

¾ yard of fabric for binding

8 yards of fabric for backing and hanging sleeve (or 3¼ yards of 110"-wide fabric)

91" x 108" piece of batting

Purchase an additional ½ to ¾ yard if you intend to "fussy cut" any pieces.

Cutting

PIECE	FABRIC	NUMBER TO CUT	SIZE
A	Focal print	12 strips	2" x 42"; crosscut into 240 squares, 2" x 2"
B	Focal print	2 strips	3½" x 42"; crosscut into 20 squares, 3½" x 3½"
C	Light background print	20 strips	2" x 42"; crosscut into 80 rectangles, 2" x 9½"
D	Light background print	14 strips	2" x 42"; crosscut into 80 rectangles, 2" x 6½"
E	Light background print	8 strips	2" x 42"; crosscut into 80 rectangles, 2" x 3½"
Side setting triangles	Focal print	4 squares	18¼" x 18¼"; cut twice diagonally to yield 16 triangles. You will have 2 left over.
Corner setting triangle	Focal print	2 squares	9⅜" x 9⅜"; cut once diagonally to yield 4 triangles
Inner borders	Contrasting print	8 strips	4 strips, 2" x 39", from the lengthwise grain; and 4 strips, 2" x 48", from the lengthwise grain
Top and bottom borders	Coordinating print	2 strips	8½" x 92", from the lengthwise grain
Side borders	Coordinating print	2 strips	8½" x 109", from the lengthwise grain
Binding	Binding fabric	10 strips	2¼" x 42"

Sewing

1. Make 12 blocks of your choice from the block gallery. Use the fat quarters, fat eighths, and fabrics from your stash to create a scrappy look. Incorporate some of the focal print in your blocks—about ½ yard has been allotted for the blocks.

2. Make the Stairway to Heaven alternate blocks by sewing two focal print A squares to opposite ends of a light background C rectangle. In the same manner, sew A squares to both ends the light background D and E rectangles as shown. Make 40 of each.

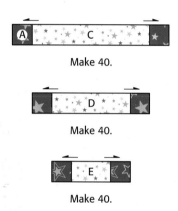

Make 40.

Make 40.

Make 40.

3. Sew together the units from step 2, the focal print B square, and the remaining light background C, D, and E rectangles as shown. Make 20 blocks.

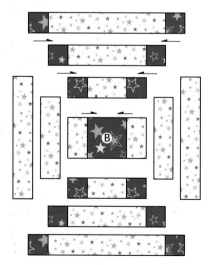

Make 20.

4. Sew the quilt top together in diagonal rows. Alternate the pieced blocks with the Stairway to Heaven blocks and add the setting triangles as shown. Press the seams toward the Stairway to Heaven blocks.

5. Join the diagonal rows, matching the seam lines as you stitch.

6. Sew two 48" inner-border strips together for one side border and press the seams open. Repeat. Sew two 39" strips together for the top border and press the seams open. Repeat for the bottom border. Sew the inner borders to the quilt top, mitering the corners. Refer to "Mitered Borders" (page 15).

7. Add the outer borders, mitering the corners.

Finishing the Quilt

Refer to "Finishing" (pages 16–18) for details on the following steps.

1. Prepare the backing and layer the quilt top, batting, and backing. Baste.

2. Quilt by hand or machine as desired and bind the quilt.

3. Make and add a hanging sleeve and label.

Made by Rosemary Makhan. Quilted by Sue Patten.

Quilt size: 63" x 75" • Finished block: 12"

I wanted all the blocks to be the same in this quilt. Using the Road to Paradise block with different fabrics in the corners creates a secondary pattern in between the stars. Choose a beautiful floral fabric for the borders and use this fabric as a guide when selecting fabrics for the blocks. I chose these fabrics because I imagine paradise as a beautiful sun-filled garden where the paths are strewn with rose petals. This quilt is bright and colorful but very soothing to the soul.

Materials

See page 79 for yardages needed for a larger quilt.

3½ yards of large-scale floral print for blocks (piece A), border, and binding

2 yards of small-scale floral background print for blocks (pieces A and B)

1¼ yards (1¾ yards for paper piecing) of pink pin-dot fabric for blocks (piece C)

⅝ yard of yellow-and-pink marbled fabric for blocks (piece A)

½ yard of small-scale yellow print for blocks (piece D)

⅜ yard of blue tone-on-tone print for blocks (piece E)

4½ yards of fabric for backing

67" x 79" piece of batting

Cutting the Blocks

Cut the block pieces referring to the Road to Paradise block (page 53). Cut enough for 20 blocks. Note that half of the outer A pieces should be cut from the large-scale floral print and half from the yellow-and-pink marbled fabric.

Sewing

1. Sew the blocks following the sewing directions for Road to Paradise (page 54). It is best to press the seams open when joining the units to make each block. This helps when sewing the blocks together to make the quilt top because it distributes the bulk more evenly.

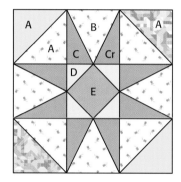

2. Stitch the blocks together in vertical rows. Press the joining seams open.

Cutting the Borders and Binding

PIECE	FABRIC	NUMBER TO CUT	SIZE
Borders	Large-scale floral print	2 strips	8" x 68", from the lengthwise grain
		2 strips	8" x 80", from the lengthwise grain
Binding	Large-scale floral print	4 strips	2¼" x 80", from the lengthwise grain

3. Join the vertical rows. Press the seams open.

4. Sew on the borders referring to "Mitered Borders" (page 15).

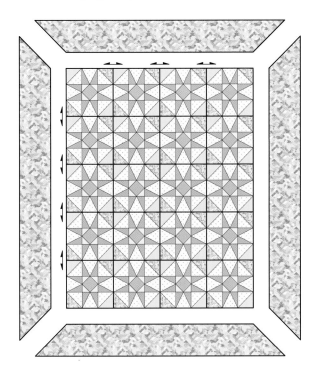

Finishing the Quilt

Refer to "Finishing" (pages 16–18) for details on the following steps.

1. Prepare the backing and layer the quilt top, batting, and backing. Baste.

2. Quilt by hand or machine as desired and bind the quilt.

3. Make and add a hanging sleeve and label.

◇

Glad Tidings

Piece the backing so that the seams go sideways— this will be the most economical use of your fabric.

◇

30-Block Quilt

Size: 75" x 87"

If you'd like to make a larger version of this quilt, you'll need fabric as listed below.

Materials

4 yards of large-scale floral print for blocks (piece A), border, and binding

3 yards of small-scale floral background print for blocks (pieces A and B)

1⅝ yards (1⅞ yards for paper piecing) of pink pin-dot fabric for blocks (piece C)

¾ yard of yellow-and-pink marbled fabric for blocks (piece A)

⅝ yard of small-scale yellow print for blocks (piece D)

½ yard of blue tone-on-tone print for blocks (piece E)

5½ yards of fabric for backing

79" x 91" piece of batting

Cut and piece 30 blocks, referring to Road to Paradise (page 53). Cut half of the outer A pieces from the large-scale floral, and half from the yellow-and-pink marbled fabric. Cut two border strips 8" x 80" and two border strips 8" x 92" from the lengthwise grain.

COAT OF MANY COLORS QUILT

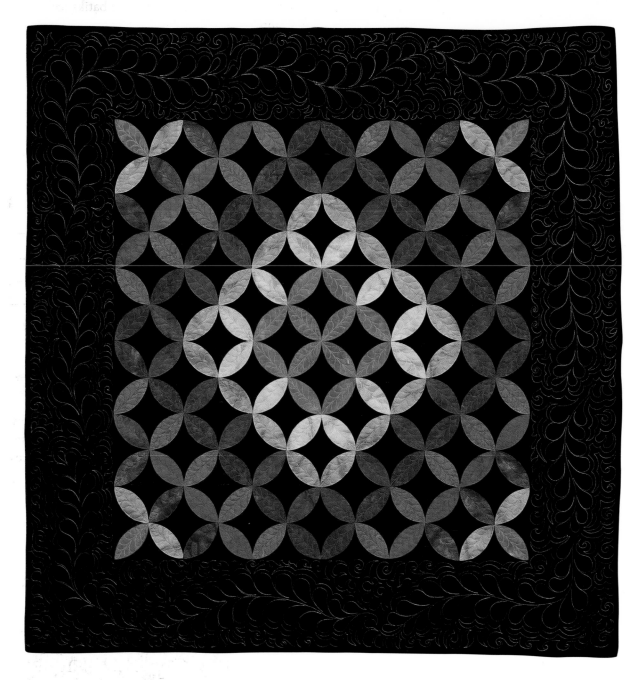

Made by Rosemary Makhan. Machine quilted by Sue Patten.

Quilt size: 50" x 50" • Finished unit: 6"

*T*he appliquéd block unit I used in this quilt is called Joseph's Coat, but it is very different from the pieced block of the same name on page 48. This appliquéd block is very simple and easy to do—it is the color variations in the fabrics that give this quilt its beauty and remind me of antique Amish quilts. Batiks or hand-dyed fabrics sparkle against the black background of this quilt.

Materials

3 yards of black fabric for top, borders, and binding

½ yard of purple batik for appliqués

1 fat quarter *each* of red-orange, green, light purple, and fuchsia batiks for appliqués

1 fat eighth *each* of gold and blue batiks for appliqués

3¼ yards of fabric for backing

54" x 54" piece of batting

Freezer paper

White chalk pencil

Cutting

PIECE	FABRIC	NUMBER TO CUT	SIZE
Background	Black	1 square	40" x 40"
Border	Black	4 strips	7½" x 55", from the lengthwise grain
Binding	Black	4 strips	2¼" x 58", from the lengthwise grain

Preparing the Appliqués

Refer to the "Freezer-Paper Appliqué" (page 13).

1. Trace the appliqué pattern on page 82 onto freezer paper. Trace and cut 144 pieces. Cut right on the marked line; four of these shapes should fit perfectly into a 6" x 6" block grid.

2. Press the freezer-paper shapes to the wrong side of the appliqué fabrics. Make 16 red-orange, 12 gold, 24 green, 44 purple, 20 light purple, 16 fuchsia, and 12 blue appliqué shapes.

3. Cut out all the appliqué pieces leaving ¼" seam allowances around the edges of the freezer-paper shapes.

4. Glue the curved edges of all the appliqué shapes and turn under along the edge of the freezer paper.

Sewing

1. Fold the 40" x 40" background fabric into quarters and gently crease to find the center.

2. Using the center and the crease lines as starting guides, lightly mark off a grid with a white chalk pencil. The grid consists of 36 squares that each measure 6" x 6".

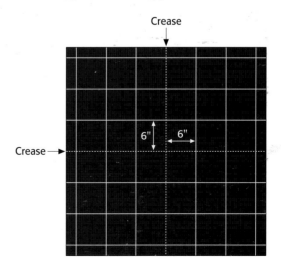

Glad Tidings

I use a white chalk pencil to mark the grid because the marks show up well and wipe off easily with a damp cloth after the stitching is finished.

3. Starting in the center of the quilt, glue in place four red-orange appliqué pieces. Place each shape on the diagonal so that the points are touching in the center as shown. Referring to the photo (page 80) and the quilt diagram at right, glue the remaining appliqué pieces in place. Pin if desired.

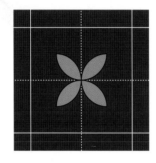

4. Stitch the appliqué pieces in place by hand or with invisible machine appliqué.

5. Trim the quilt top, leaving a ¼" seam allowance all around the edge of the appliqué shapes. Align the ¼" line of a long ruler with the chalk line.

6. Add the borders, referring to "Mitered Borders" (page 15).

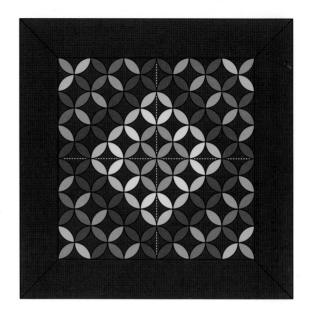

Finishing the Quilt

Refer to "Finishing" (pages 16–18) for details on the following steps.

1. Prepare the backing and layer the quilt top, batting, and backing. Baste.

2. Quilt by hand or machine as desired and bind the quilt.

3. Make and add a hanging sleeve and label.

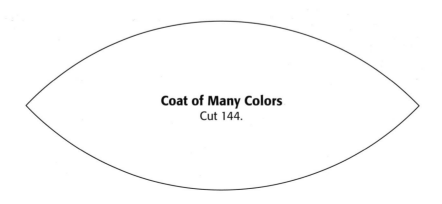

Coat of Many Colors
Cut 144.

Made by Rosemary Makhan. Machine quilted by Sue Patten.

Quilt size: 43½" x 43½" • Finished block: 9"

*T*he classic Jacob's Ladder block lends itself to a multitude of variations when you place colors selectively as I did in this quilt. I shaded the fabrics so there appears to be a light source in the center of the quilt. The piecing is very easy, but the result is striking. This quilt was inspired by my love of antique Amish quilts.

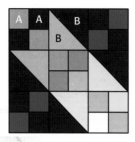

Jacob's Ladder

Materials

1½ yards of dark purple for borders and binding

1⅛ yards of black for blocks

1 fat eighth *each* of cream, yellow, light purple, medium purple, dark purple, light pink, medium pink, medium burgundy, dark burgundy, aqua, turquoise, very light blue, light blue, medium blue and light green for blocks

1 fat quarter *each* of fuchsia, medium green, dark green and dark blue for blocks

2¾ yards of fabric for backing (or 1½ yards of 60"-wide backing fabric)

47" x 47" piece of batting

Cutting

PIECE	FABRIC	NUMBER TO CUT	SIZE
A	Yellow and cream	4 squares of *each* color	2" x 2"
	Light purple, medium purple, light pink, and medium pink	6 squares of *each* color	2" x 2"
	Aqua and light green	8 squares of *each* color	2" x 2"
	Medium burgundy and dark burgundy	12 squares of *each* color	2" x 2"
	Turquoise	16 squares	2" x 2"
	Dark purple and fuchsia	24 squares of *each* color	2" x 2"
	Medium green	28 squares	2" x 2"
	Dark green	36 squares	2" x 2"
	Black	128 squares	2" x 2"
B	Black	32 squares	3⅞" x 3⅞"; cut once diagonally to yield 64 triangles
	Very light blue	4 squares	3⅞" x 3⅞"; cut once diagonally to yield 8 triangles
	Light blue and medium blue	8 squares of *each* color	3⅞" x 3⅞", cut once diagonally to yield 16 light blue and 16 medium blue triangles
	Dark blue	12 squares	3⅞" x 3⅞"; cut once diagonally to yield 24 triangles
Borders*	Dark purple	2 strips	4¼" x 38", from the lengthwise grain
		2 strips	4¼" x 46", from the lengthwise grain
Binding	Dark green	4 strips	2¼" x 48", from the lengthwise grain

The borders are cut slightly longer than needed and will be trimmed after stitching.

Sewing the Blocks

For each block, sew the A pieces together into four-patch units and the B pieces into triangle-square units. Join them into three rows and join the rows. Keep track of the block numbers by pinning a number to each block as you complete it.

1. Make four different center blocks as shown. These are blocks 6, 7, 10, and 11.

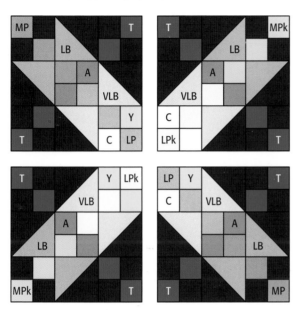

Make 1 each for center.

2. Make two blocks as shown for blocks 5 and 12.

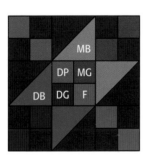

Make 2.

3. Make two blocks as shown for blocks 8 and 9.

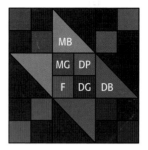

Make 2.

4. Make two blocks as shown for blocks 2 and 15.

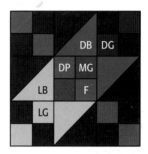

Make 2.

5. Make two blocks as shown for blocks 3 and 14.

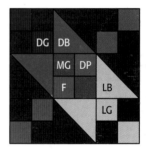

Make 2.

Color Key

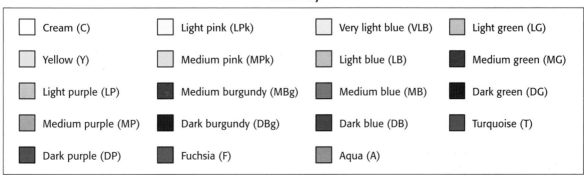

Cream (C)	Light pink (LPk)	Very light blue (VLB)	Light green (LG)
Yellow (Y)	Medium pink (MPk)	Light blue (LB)	Medium green (MG)
Light purple (LP)	Medium burgundy (MBg)	Medium blue (MB)	Dark green (DG)
Medium purple (MP)	Dark burgundy (DBg)	Dark blue (DB)	Turquoise (T)
Dark purple (DP)	Fuchsia (F)	Aqua (A)	

6. Make four corner blocks as shown. These are blocks 1, 4, 13, and 16.

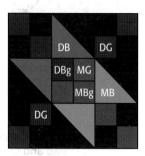

Make 4 corner blocks.

Assembling the Quilt

1. Lay out the blocks, paying particular attention to the direction and position of each block. Refer to the numbered diagram below for correct placement.

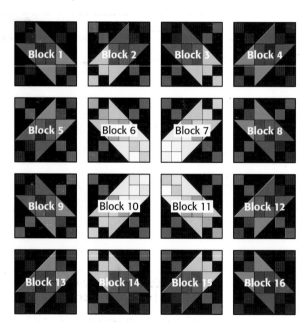

2. Join the blocks together into four vertical rows. Join the rows.

3. Add the borders, referring to "Straight-Cut Borders" (page 14).

Finishing the Quilt

Refer to "Finishing" (pages 16–18) for details on the following steps.

1. Prepare the backing and layer the quilt top, batting, and backing. Baste.

2. Quilt by hand or machine as desired and bind the quilt.

3. Make and add a hanging sleeve and label.

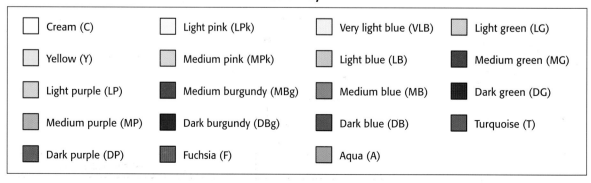

Color Key

Cream (C)	Light pink (LPk)	Very light blue (VLB)	Light green (LG)
Yellow (Y)	Medium pink (MPk)	Light blue (LB)	Medium green (MG)
Light purple (LP)	Medium burgundy (MBg)	Medium blue (MB)	Dark green (DG)
Medium purple (MP)	Dark burgundy (DBg)	Dark blue (DB)	Turquoise (T)
Dark purple (DP)	Fuchsia (F)	Aqua (A)	

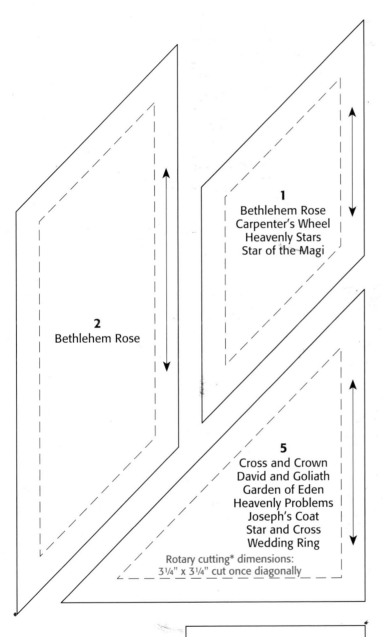

1
Bethlehem Rose
Carpenter's Wheel
Heavenly Stars
Star of the Magi

2
Bethlehem Rose

5
Cross and Crown
David and Goliath
Garden of Eden
Heavenly Problems
Joseph's Coat
Star and Cross
Wedding Ring

Rotary cutting* dimensions:
3¼" x 3¼" cut once diagonally

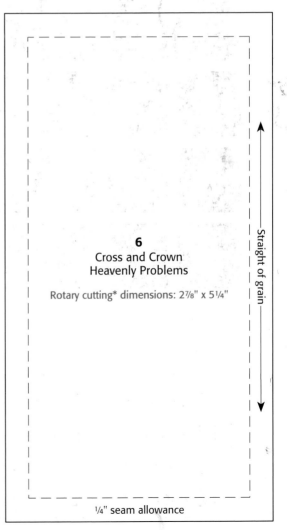

4
Cross and Crown
David and Goliath
Garden of Eden
Heavenly Problems
Joseph's Coat
Star and Cross
Wedding Ring

Rotary cutting* dimensions: 2⅞" x 2⅞"

6
Cross and Crown
Heavenly Problems

Rotary cutting* dimensions: 2⅞" x 5¼"

Straight of grain

¼" seam allowance

*If you choose to rotary cut, your blocks will finish at 11⅞" rather than 12". Most quilters do not have a problem with this small difference in block size.

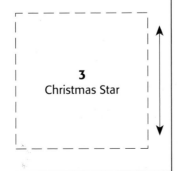

3
Christmas Star

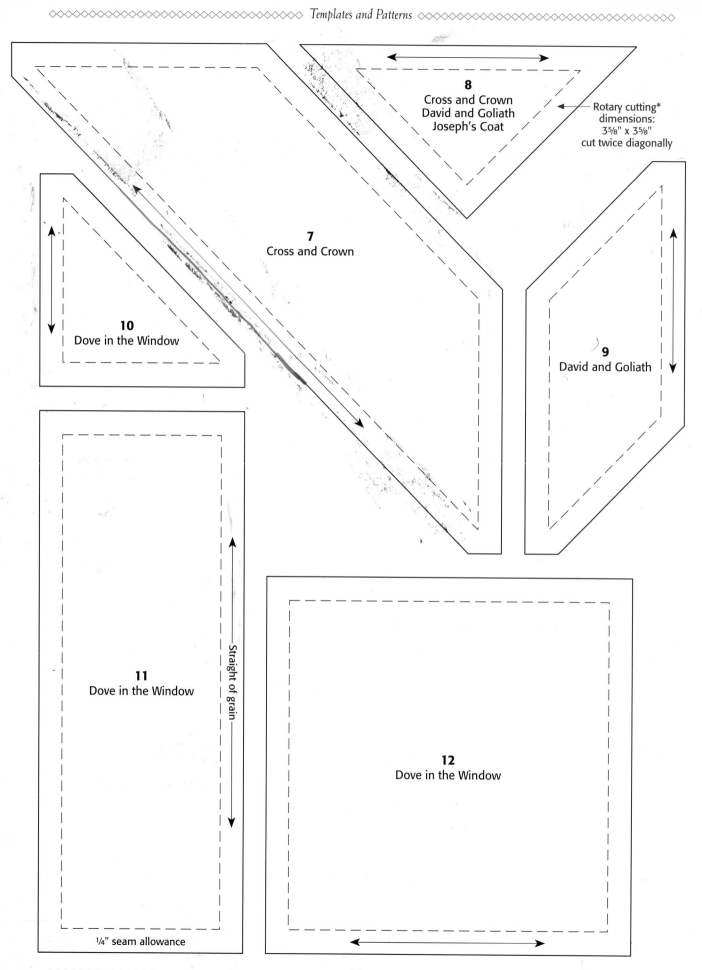

8
Cross and Crown
David and Goliath
Joseph's Coat

Rotary cutting*
dimensions:
3⅝" x 3⅝"
cut twice diagonally

7
Cross and Crown

10
Dove in the Window

9
David and Goliath

11
Dove in the Window

Straight of grain

12
Dove in the Window

¼" seam allowance

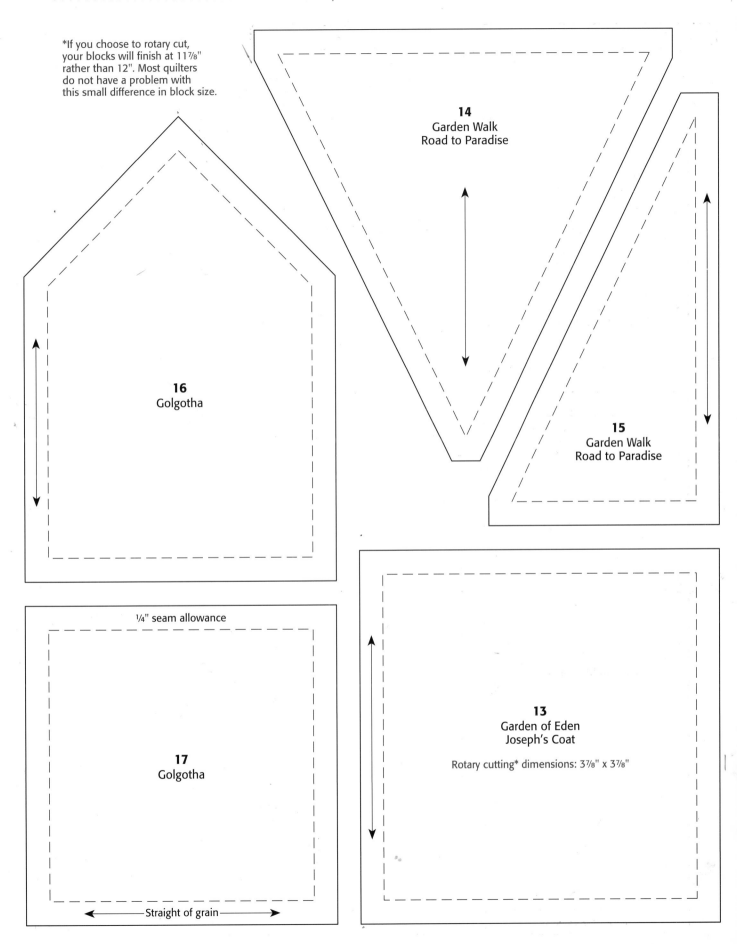

*If you choose to rotary cut, your blocks will finish at 11⅞" rather than 12". Most quilters do not have a problem with this small difference in block size.

14
Garden Walk
Road to Paradise

16
Golgotha

15
Garden Walk
Road to Paradise

¼" seam allowance

17
Golgotha

←—— Straight of grain ——→

13
Garden of Eden
Joseph's Coat

Rotary cutting* dimensions: 3⅞" x 3⅞"

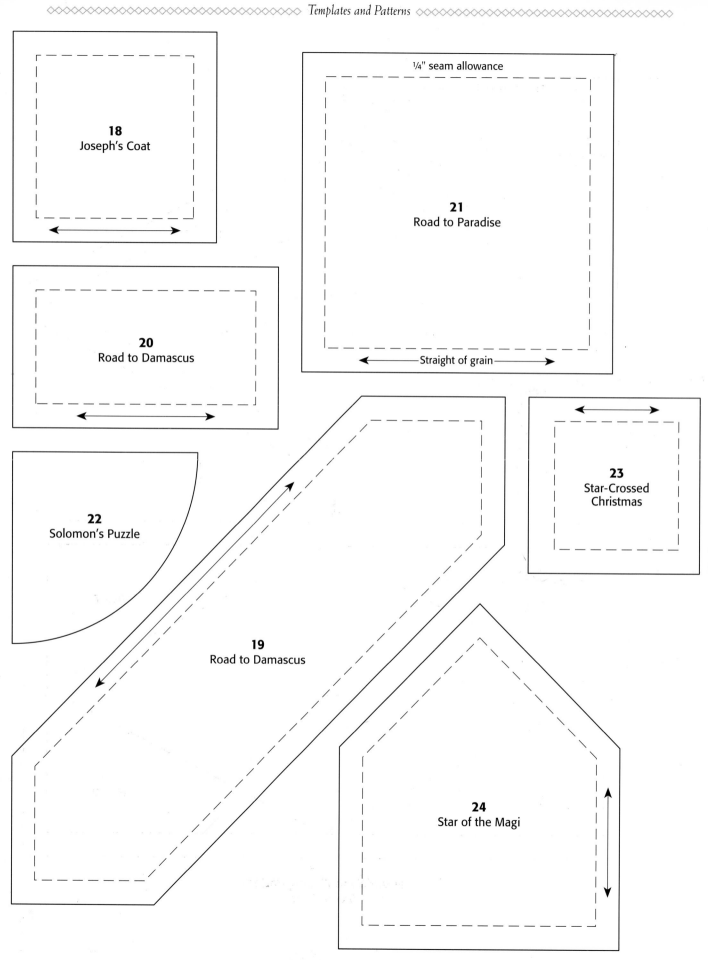

18
Joseph's Coat

¼" seam allowance

21
Road to Paradise

Straight of grain

20
Road to Damascus

22
Solomon's Puzzle

23
Star-Crossed
Christmas

19
Road to Damascus

24
Star of the Magi

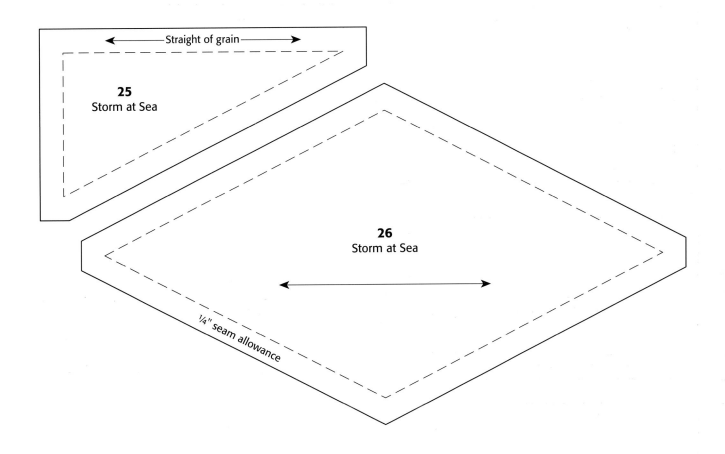

25
Storm at Sea

26
Storm at Sea

Straight of grain

¼" seam allowance

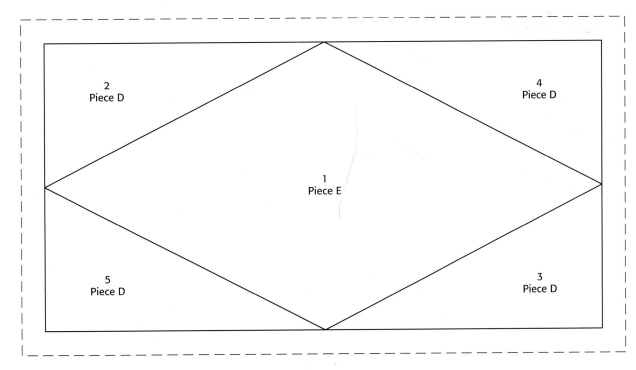

2
Piece D

4
Piece D

1
Piece E

5
Piece D

3
Piece D

Foundation Piecing Pattern
Storm at Sea

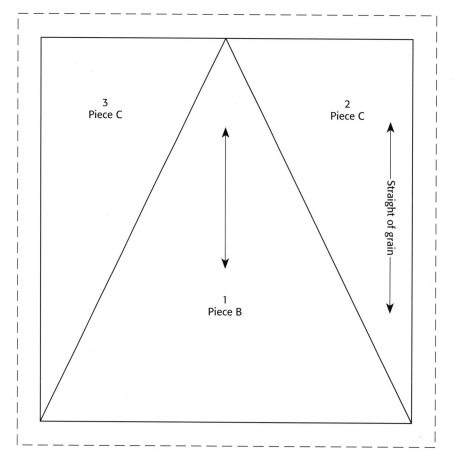

Foundation Piecing Pattern
Garden Walk
Road to Paradise

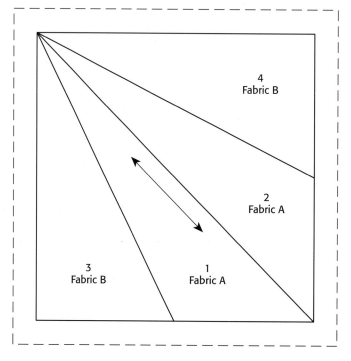

Foundation Piecing Pattern
Job's Troubles

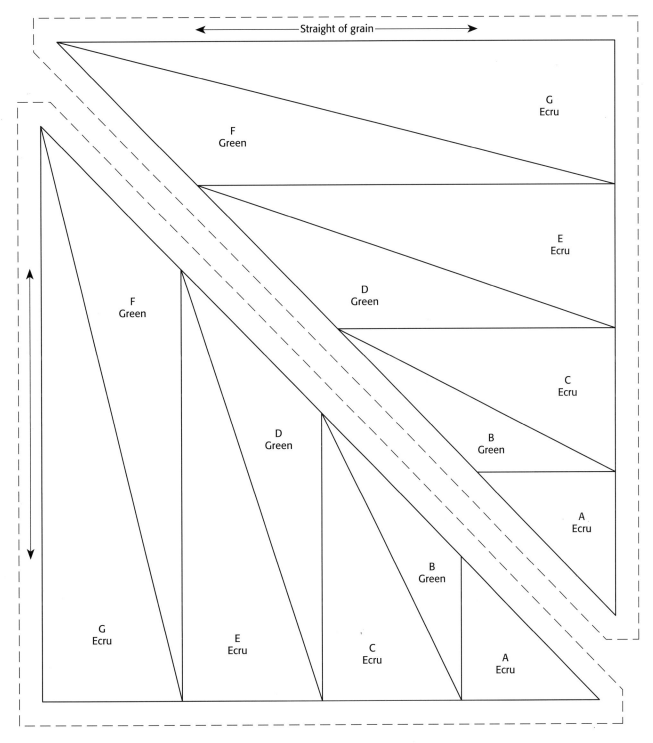

Foundation Piecing Patterns
Hosanna

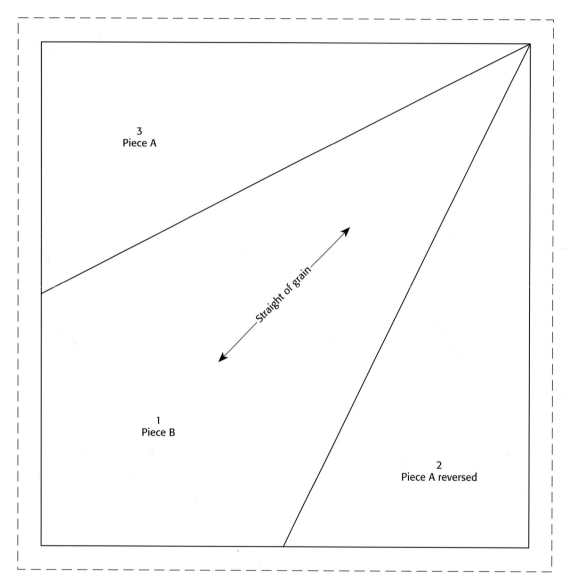

Foundation Piecing Pattern
King David's Crown

BIBLIOGRAPHY

Doak, Carol. *Show Me How to Paper Piece*. Woodinville, Wash.: Martingale & Company, 1997.

Eppler, Roxi. *Smoothstitch Quilts*. Woodinville, Wash.: Martingale & Company, 1993.

Makhan, Rosemary. *Biblical Blocks*. Woodinville, Wash.: Martingale & Company, 2001.

Makhan, Rosemary. *Floral Abundance*. Woodinville, Wash.: Martingale & Company, 2000.

RESOURCES

International Textiles Ltd.
8811 Beckwith Road
Richmond, British Columbia, Canada V6X 1V4

O-Pal shaded appliqué fabrics used in "Coat of Many Colors"

Patten That Quilt, Inc.
641 Phoebe Crescent
Burlington, Ontario, Canada L7L 6H8

Beautiful long-arm machine quilting on "Coat of Many Colors Quilt," "30-Block Sampler," "Road to Paradise Quilt," and "Jacob's Ladder Quilt"

SewUnique
40 Gulch Road
Sheridan, WY 82801

Quilter's Quarter Marker

G&S Dye and Accessories Ltd.
250 Dundas St. W, Unit 8
Toronto, Ontario, Canada M5T 2Z5

Raycafix dye fixative

Telio & Cie
5800 St. Denis, Suite 502
Montreal, Quebec, Canada H3S 3L5

Mist tone-on-tone black fabric used in "Coat of Many Colors"

Rosemary Makhan grew up in Nova Scotia, Canada, where she learned the basics of quiltmaking from her mother. Her love of sewing and fabric led her to major in home economics at Nova Scotia Teachers College and at Acadia University. She taught high school family studies for several years.

Her interest in quiltmaking was rekindled when she made a baby quilt for her daughter, Candice, who likes to tell her friends that, if it weren't for her, her mother probably wouldn't have begun her quiltmaking career.

Rosemary taught adult education classes, becoming the founding president of the Halton Quilters Guild in 1977. She continues to teach many quiltmaking classes and workshops and enjoys the special fellowship and inspiration that come from working with quilters.

A traditional quiltmaker, Rosemary loves appliqué and makes many pieced quilts as well. She especially loves sampler quilts that are based on a theme, such as her *Biblical Blocks, Samplings from the Sea, Rose Sampler Supreme,* and *Make Mine Country* quilts. Often, the quilts she makes are her own design. If they are not, she changes or adds something to make them distinctive. She has created many patterns, including the popular Woodland Creature Collector Series, printed under her pattern label, Quilts by Rosemary.

Each fall, Rosemary helps conduct a Quilting in the Country retreat for quilters in the picturesque Ontario countryside. She now lives in Burlington, Ontario, Canada, with her husband, Chris. They have a daughter, Candice. Their son, Kenneth, developed schizophrenia at the age of 23, and passed away suddenly in his sleep due to an interaction of medications two years later.

To see more of Rosemary's quilts, visit her website: www.quiltsbyrosemary.com.